# new poems
# for
# Labour

An anthology of poems
written by members of the Labour Party
reflecting their political disappointments
and aspirations as we approach the end
of the century and the end of a
disastrous spell of Tory rule.

compiled by Derek Alan Taylor
Secretary of Stafford Labour Party

with a foreword by
Rt. Hon. Roy Hattersley M.P.

Proceeds will help Labour win

Published by the Compiler at
7 Old Acre Lane, Brocton, STAFFORD ST17 0TW
Printed by Counterprint, Tipping Street, STAFFORD ST16 2LL

To my parents
Bob and Lilian Taylor
formerly of Lambeth
for giving me a vision,
and to Sylvia
a wonderful companion
wife and mother

# Compiler's Note

The inspiration for this book of poems came from none other than that great Scottish Bard, Robert Burns. A few years ago I had the pleasure of joining the company of a Scot, named Andy Smith during an enlightening visit to Russia (before the recent decline into capitalism). After that trip, on a visit to his home in Aberdeen, Andy introduced me to Burns' "A man's a man for a' that". Of course, I had read it before, but his description of the circumstances under which it was first delivered and his Scottish rendering gave it new meaning.

Apparently Burns, who had become a notable (though still poor) poet, was asked to write a piece for the occasion of a banquet given by the local Laird, and he was invited along to deliver it. Read it again, and you too will appreciate its true significance. Imagine the scene! an almost medieval assemblage of the most important Scottish landowners and aristocrats, and Burns stood up and effectively told them that they were men of little minds, "coofs" (fools), that their rank was "but the guinea's stamp, the man's the gold for a' that", that the honest man was above their might, and that the man of independent mind "looks and laughs at a' that".

The commemoration of his untimely passing 200 years ago led me to look closer at Burns' life and works, and it was in doing this that I came to realise how political many of his other poems were. One, called Awa' Whigs Awa', inspired me to write a variation (Awa' Cons Awa'). Then the Post Office decided to commemorate the bicentenary of his death, so I wrote the piece "First Class - Post" to say thank you. It was only then that it occurred to me how relevant it would be to publish a book of topical political verse, and where better to seek this anthology than among ordinary Labour Party members. If we can raise some much needed funding in the process, so much the better.

A letter in the Labour Party News brought a totally unexpected response. I received almost 500 poems in a matter of weeks. When I started this thing, I don't think I really believed that anything would come of it, but circumstances and fellow socialists have inspired me to completion.

In making the selection, I have not always gone for the "best poetry". For one thing, I do not consider myself qualified to make such a choice. In any case this is so subjective a matter that in a collection of this kind it would not be sensible. In many cases what some would regard as poor poetry comes alive because of the sincerity of the emotions expressed. It is apparent that much of the work has been inspired by real experiences. I hope it gives the reader as much pleasure as I have had in putting it all together.

I have not applied any form of classification - the subject matter is too varied to make that worthwhile - but I have attempted a degree of indexing to help the reader find, and re-find particular poems.

I am deeply indebted to all the contributors for the many hours they have put in to the work, and to that veteran of culture, Roy Hattersley for agreeing to write the foreword.

It is with deep regret that I have to report that during the production of this book, two of our contributors, Jim Owen of Blackpool and Neville Frohock of Lincoln, have passed away. I hope the publication of their poems will give some comfort to the loved ones they leave behind.

*Derek Alan Taylor*
*Stafford, September 1996*

# Foreword

by Rt. Hon. Roy Hattersley M.P.

The title is important. It is the poems that are New and very few of them reflect an abandonment of Labour's old beliefs or a rejection of Labour's history. Of course, the anthology is written by men and women who are desperate for a New Labour victory. But poetry, by its nature, links memories of the past with hopes for the future. So Jean Cardy's *Suffragette* *(p150)* — expected to fight old battles — announces

> That's all a long time ago.
> It's the future I care about.

Anyone who reads Jean Cardy's poems - one of the more prolific authors in the anthology - will marvel at the breadth of her interests and the extent of her activities.

> I feel guilty
> When I attack ants with kettles of boiling water
> and puffer packs of poison.          *(Ants-p179)*

For me, at least, it is impossible not to wonder why she does it. Certainly it is not a habit she enjoys. But the poem suggests that a day rarely passes without her lifting a stone and seeing

> the cracked tunnels and rows of dead eggs.

Perhaps It is just the poetic imagination at work to illustrate the feelings of the men and women whose lives have been destroyed during the last seventeen years.

Folk memories almost invariably produce bitter resentment. Patricia Riley *(p38)* remembers

> Our great-grandfather, William, died at 38,
> Down the pit.
> An accidental fall of stone...

The irony with which the poem ends,

> Nothing like that ever happens today,
> Of course not! How could it?

illustrates one of the great dilemmas of bringing socialism up to date. All of us who were brought up in mining areas know the ambition to keep sons out of the collieries. Most of us demonstrated at some time over the past ten years about pit closures. Perhaps there is a paradox. One of poetry's purposes is to reveal complicated truths by constructing such complicated contradictions.

With the most ironic poems, the joke is usually on the Labour Party itself. Party meeting *(p89)*, by Gavin Ross, is all we know and all we need to know about a local branch agenda. The resolution calls

> ...upon the Party, at some date or other...
> to create a socialist economy...

The assembled socialists

> ...Vote. It's passed nem con.

And they believe

> We've done our bit.

Sabrina Doyle, declaring *Not Just Nostalgia (p66)*, begins "Socialism is Dead".

Her comparison is

> a young girl whose picture he used to keep in his wallet a long long time ago...

No it is not! Not while socialists go on writing poems of the quality that Derek Taylor has collected. If there is a criticism to be made of New Poems for Labour it is that proper bitterness about what has gone on since 1979 often drives out the joy which is supposed to go with socialism. But that will come if a volume of poems is produced after the 1997 election.

Back in 1948, a dozen lines of doggerel appeared in a school magazine. They began:

> They might've done much better
> But they might've done much worse.
> It's gone from t'rich man's pocket,
> But it's in the poor man's purse.

The rest I forget. But it was a celebration of three years of Labour government. I hope the Blair administration will justify more unqualified praise, than I offered to Mr Attlee over forty years ago. I hope too it will inspire another volume of New Poems for a Labour government.

*Roy Hattersley*

# New Poems for Labour

## New Labour

Let this book of poems lift hearts into Labour.
Show the leaders the way for honest politics
Give our people justice, make them a family,
Give advice, when needed.
Hold hands and bring people opportunity
and equality!

*Kenneth Mood*
*Blaydon CLP*

## The Old Age Pensioner

I'm just an old age pensioner
But do the Tories care?
And like that famous lady
I've not a thing to wear

I wonder "Can I buy that chop?",
For in the shops there's plenty
Alas when I look in my purse
I find that it is empty.

The answer to our problems
Is really very clear:
Just put your cross for LABOUR
Get the Tories out of here!

*Nellie Rogers (Aged 84)*
*Edinburgh Central CLP*

## Reducing the Stock

When Major stands applauding,
Those ministerial cooks,
His cheers for skills they all possess,
When busy cooking books,
Turns to quite ecstatic pleasure,
As tossed into the fry,
Go the remnants of those lemons,
They've previously squeezed dry.

*John O'Rourke, Wallsend*
*Teignmouth CLP*

# Stars In Their Eyes

*In '96 Bill Cash, Stafford's noted Euro-sceptic and right-winger, announced his intention of seeking a safer seat for the next election, even though Stafford had been Tory since Hugh Fraser took it in 1951. Cash was selected for nearby Stone. The new Tory candidate, aged 29, was described by the local press as the youngest ever in Stafford.*

The Tories have a bright young star
They've brought to Stafford from afar
To fight the seat that Cash defected
With little chance to get elected.
They say that he's the youngest yet,
Those Tories, how they do forget !
Or should I say "how prone they seems
To little fibs and little dreams?"

The Youngest was a Labour man
In seventy I was his fan.
Jon Stanworth – only 28
Had Frazer in a right old state.
Back then the seat was such a mix
With Tory voters in the sticks,
But now the bound'ry's been redrawn
That Tory vote has been quite shorn
And surely those that's left inside
Can see they're heading for a hide.

In '66 – four years before
Another youngster came to score
The name that time was Graham Rea
At 29 he had his day.
Unless John Major makes his cast
Before another year has passed
Yon Tory will be past his prime
The big three O will mark his time.

So, Tories, say you're sorry please
To voters you deceive with ease
And when you feel the need to shine
Just do it with an honest line.

*Derek Alan Taylor*
*Stafford LP*

## Union Rep

Brother!

There are those outside who cannot understand you.
Why should you give so much of your time
Fighting for better pay, and conditions for them?
You receive no remuneration, and very little appreciation
You do a normal day's work, and then go straight to a meeting.
You give up most of your social life,
And attend Seminars at weekends – and worry.

The management hate and despise you,
And some of your members think you're a fool.
You work hard to get your message across,
Sometimes you shout, sometimes you despair,
But you have a fighting spirit and never give up.
And beneath that tough exterior there is a soft
And caring heart.

Brother!

There are those outside who cannot understand you,
But they seek you out in times of trouble,
And then they vanish into an apathetic crowd
Of members who do nothing only pay their subs,
Sit on their backsides, and wait for the fruits
Of your efforts.
You know this, but because you are what you are
You continue to be a shop steward.

And Brother

I Salute You!

*Ron Ellis*
*Tatton CLP*

## Elegy Written In an Urban Churchyard (1995)

A bell rings out, the last bus pulls away,
Passengers off, its groan fades distantly.
A chummy group splits homeward each asway,
And leaves the world deserted but for me.

Beam down a street lamp pools its orange light,
And sleepy quiet holds the night that's cold,
'Cept where with fleeting flicker blue and bright,
A blaring siren splits the peaceful fold.

Beneath the shawl of some old weeping tree,
Against such inclemence the night won't spare,
A sudden makeshift shelter comes to be:
A cardboard hut for me and mine to share.

Then near these monuments on earthly holds,
Within yon porch's scant'ly offered lee,
A wine-soaked creature from his mouth unfolds,
Profane invective to his poverty.

The dipso-maniacal night begins,
And all this sacred plots tranquillity,
Degenerates back to our origins,
As outcasts slur aloud obscenity

Each sodden soul in dereliction there
Within the Porch's crowded sanctuary,
At night betwixt them contest who for where,
The choicest spot shall gain their tenury.

Bereft of trace of grace or self esteem,
De-humanised and cast upon the heap,
With single minded equal conduct mean,
They crave the welcome void their stoppers keep.

The fisticuffs, the breaking bottles sound,
The oaths, the blows the injuries uncared,
The drunkards defecate on cherished mounds,
And urinate upon the graven word.

Then slowly that narcosis which is night,
Quails down to flickered dormancy their fire,
And from known penury their wretched plight,
Succumbs inexorably to sleeps desire.

For them no warmth nor hope's ambitions burn,
Nor friendly auspice hold some chance that's fair;
No enterprise for self respect to earn
Nor glimmered cause dispel their dark despair.

Let not some die-hard words in language sage,
Nor confederate surly notions spoil,
Some trust eventual fortune might engage,
Emergence from their grave above the soil.

Above them on their ivy mantled tower,
The buzzards preen their cruel talons keen.
On feathered nests they concentrate their power,
To swoop from high and pick their preys bones clean.

*Epilogue*
A rumbling growl of motors on the dawn,
The groans and stirrings 'neath each hasty shed,
A grating honk impatient on a horn.
No more we transgress now. Take up thy bed.
*End*

*John O'Rourke*
*Tynemouth CLP*

## Message To Maggie (1988)

Repent ye Maggie while ye may, its nearing judgement day,
For sins you have committed for which most of us must pay.
The heartache and the suffering, the misery and strife,
The wounds are all so very deep we'll bear the scars for life.

The richest you've made richer; the poor much poorer still,
The NHS you've nigh destroyed, you're poising for the kill.
Our assets you have bartered, no compassion have you shown.
The Iron Maiden that you are, you'll reap as you have sown.

*Martha Prescott (Aged 80)*
*Scunthorpe CLP*

5

## Useful Employment

Our standard of nations that flag up a pole,
Gave heart to us all as it fluttered
And proudly upstanding with pride in our chests,
We sang loud the good song and uttered
Those words about classlessness freedom and pride,
Of our country where no one had reason,
To doubt dispensation of Justice unbiased;
That was 'til the Cons got their season.

Then down crashed all standards, out came the axe;
Compassion sailed out of the door.
They stitched up democracy – tailored for them;
Their target – the needs of the poor.
Then privatisations with jobs for the boys,
All launched on a sick sea of sleaze:
Redundancies, health cuts with quangos in power
And a permanent pong on the breeze.

Sang gloriously their faithful encores abound,
With their pockets cupped ready to line.
Their plunderbugs stacked from dowers of the poor,
To the ears of proverbial swine.
Tactics and dole queues, fork tongues and ruse
The nation got took by their trick,
'Til it wasn't just the flag they had up the pole,
Britannia got stuck up the stick.

Why do you hang there, damp rag up a pole,
Sadly bedraggled and slack
Have you like me been depowered endlessly
With their 'Right up your union Jack!' ?
Come down dear frayed old thing help me to dry
Those tears for lost dignity smarting my eye.
Come down and help me with noise to dispose,
Through useful employment what's right up my nose.

*John O'Rourke*
*Tynemouth CLP*

## Reductio Ad Absurdum

Here lies Geordie clothed in wood,
    Did like they all said he should:
Biked to London – backed a losser,
    Finished up without a tosser.

Treated like he had the pox,
    Kipping In a cardboard box,
Destitute poor Geordie sank
    (His soul's been claimed by Barclays Bank).

*John O'Rourke*
*Tynemouth CLP*

## Remembrance Day

*(In response to criticism of Michael Foot's Donkey Jacket)*

Elegance sartorial
Is the true memorial.
Remember the bleeding dead
With a bowler on your head.
Remember the mud and stink
Wrapped in your mink.
Remember the blood and pain.
Who said we died in vain?

*Sylvia Bates*
*South East Cornwall CLP*

## Keep The Red Flag Flying

Keep the red flag flying here, and try with all our might
    To give the crumbling Tories, their biggest ever fright.
One kick is all that's needed, the order of the boot,
    And demand that they return to us, all that stolen loot.

From strength to strength with might and main, to fight them
                                    tooth and nail,
    For we must not lose this one. Indeed, we must not fail!
Let's make a supreme effort, we all must try to woo
    The voters all to Labour, NOT SD or TORY blue.

*Martha Prescott*
*Scunthorpe CLP*

## At An Angle (June 1992)

Through the window
Trees reflected
Branches from one neighbour's garden
Mirrored there at an angle
In another neighbour's window.

Ignoring bricks and rooftiles
I can read the swaying never-still
And trembling beauty of the
Topmost virtual images
As if they alone are real.

Impermanent shapes
Of wandering clouds can change
The whole; only this sharp
Black-painted gutter and this drainpipe
Insist on permanence.

A gun
Lying across a muddy rut
Where a tank passed over
Before they all blew into fragments
Dealt with; dispersed.

Dead leaves
From a dying Elm
Clogging the overflow, the little weir
At angles to the lock gate,
Souping up the water.

Richness accumulates
To sickness with nowhere to turn
pain of not knowing
Where neighbour ends and I begin
Mere particles in process.

Imperceptible heat
Firing down on skin
From that clear blue sky;
Weapon to destroy, they say,
Up to twenty per cent of the population.

Jet planes landing
On decaying concrete runways
As heads of state arrive in Rio
To postpone a crumbling
Status quo.

A heavy lorry passes
Messenger of profit and loss;
Juggernaut of consummation.
The gutter-drainpipe angle shudders
At the shaking of foundations.

*Sonia Greger*
*Crewe & Nantwich CLP*

## Desertification

We have not met
you and you and you and I
Perhaps disparate
each of us feels alone;
But know that we are waiting

closed in
like desert plants
surviving long drought
inside the finished body
of the mother.

Then comes the rain
Dry cells swell
and open to free
their seeds. New life
pours out in glory.

So we, in arid times
and fear of great destruction
close quiet in hope
and seem to die;
but know that we are waiting.

*Sonia Greger*
*Crewe & Nantwich CLP*

## Tommorow's World

Tomorrow's world, what do we see?
Not much hope but misery.
Nuclear war on the horizon looms
Hurtling us towards our tombs.

Killing everything in sight,
Creatures all, and birds in flight,
Laying bare green pleasant lands
Leaving cold, barren desert sands.

So let us pause upon the brink
Before we fall and finally sink
Into oblivion, with no return,
This planet to explode and burn.

*Martha Prescott (Aged 80)*
*Scunthorpe CLP*

## The Homeless

Come with me and see where the down and outs are sleeping
'Neath newspapers and tattered rags their freezing toes are peeping
The frost and fog, the biting winds, and relentless rain
They're all resigned to what's doled out, it's useless to complain.

It's scandalous in this era of progress and of speed,
That there isn't any shelter for those who are in need.
That they have nowhere to sleep, but on the cold bare earth
Whilst those endowed with life's riches don't know just what
they're worth.

There are young ones and old ones, women and men
The "dregs of humanity" who really don't know when
Will a caring hand be given to raise them out the mire
Of utter degradation, there's so much to desire.

Huddled 'gainst the gratings, a little warmth to get,
Sometimes they are hungry, and sometimes they are wet.
Curled up for shelter 'gainst the weather that's so cold,
Rejected and dejected, full of misery untold!

*Martha Prescott*
*Scunthorpe CLP*

# Family Values

Free market family nobody cares
  Walking the tightrope of success and despair
Out of work husband told "the state is corruptive"
  Yet who will look after the 'economically inactive'?

Labelled child placed on probation
  For Internalising the values of a free market educa-
  tion.
One parent daughter forced to submit
  To a life full of hardship on reduced benefit.

Overworked mother absorbing the effects
  Of free market ravages that theorists neglect.
Societal breakdown, (but don't question the culture
  Of market place values or the Capitalist vulture).

Blame the people, dismantle the State
  Drown us with ideology of how to make Britain great.
But who pays the price of free market greed?
  Those at the top, or those in need?

It's the free market family for whom nobody cares
  Walking the tightrope of success and despair.

*Mark George*
*East Ham CLP*

# Down And Out

His trousers are huge with paper
Which occasionally filters out
Into the gutter.
He bends and patiently replaces it,
Stuffing the great sad toy
Which is himself.

No-one sees his face
As he squats his bulk
By the church door.

We pass by in another world.

*Fred Finney*
*City of York CLP*

## Radical Memories

Time is a'fleeting, old bones are a'creaking
But nothing can erase fond memories,
Of old comrades loyal, now peacefully sleeping
All gone with my yesterdays.

They fought hard to end dire poverty's scourge
Enduring the barbs of the fight.
They gave hope to all when faith they would urge
In the struggle to change wrong to right.

Radical memories reach out to the past
To the heroes who sought no reward.
Whether winning or losing, we all stood steadfast,
Disdaining the bullet or sword.

That era has gone, but still we fight on
With millions in poverty's trap,
While the affluent rich keep sponging along
Like fat cat's in Luxury's lap.

*Annie Mackie OBE (aged 90)*
*Kilmarnock & Loudoun CLP*

## A Strong Constitution

*Following the TV interview with Diana. A 'constitutional expert' said*
*'we have no written constitution – we make it up as we go'.*

A written Constitution?
What a load of bunk.
We have a firm Establishment,
The centuries have not sunk.
The rights we have unwritten
They wrote to keep control,
Their comfortable minority,
First always past the poll.
Why rewrite unwritten rights,
As lesser countries wrote?
Just doff your cap politely,
And learn your rights by rote.

*D A Clapp*
*Horsham LP*

## Highland Hymn
## (Waombh-Or'ainn Aigha'idhealtachd)

*(On the clearances on the Isle of Lewis– Pay the rent,
Emigrate, Join the Army, or bloody starve)*

From the great glen striding northwards
To Islands westward o'er the sea,
The faint stirrings of our people
Tired of the ways that be.
Tired of being political nothings
Tired of Ministerial shunts
Crying "Who on earth will save us
From these secretarial stunts".

Och the Macs and Wics forever
Represent a fighting force
We must push and pull together
To maintain our mountain source
This our children all must sing –
Of days that once will come again
And our Highland hymn's triumphant ring
Despite the sorrow and pain.

*(Macs and Wics = "Sons of" and "Daughters of")*
*Macille Mhoire*
*Yeovil CLP*

## Aspire

Pennies to restore God's house
a modest contribution
to save a threatened sanctuary
of hollowed stone and mellowed light
for thoughts serene. But I'm bewildered
by the vision of the goal
a thirty foot thermometer
with cash flow rising up the steeple
like an excitable temperature.
The church is a potent symbol, true
but is that glorious spire bent
on heaven, the jackpot or a bout of 'flu?

*Gabriel Chanan*
*Windsor CLP*

## For The People

If democracy is by the people, then where did they go wrong,
Were they just simple minded when they needed to be strong?
Four times they marked their crosses, and enough of them
                                            chose blue
Which meant that the majority just had to struggle through.

With Tory dogma at the helm, Free markets in full flow,
Trade Unions were hamstrung, and jobs began to go.
Many felt the impact, a few remained immune.
It helped if you were wealthy as the Tories called the tune.

Social fairness disappeared, unemployment lists grew longer.
The poor and homeless felt the squeeze as the Tory grip closed
                                            stronger.
De-regulate and privatise, that was their commons cry,
And as the rich grew richer, the rest of us stood by.

If democracy's of the people, then how could this be right
But if we are to change things,
            IT'S THE PEOPLE WE MUST FIGHT!

*R Pearson*
*Leeds East CLP*

## The Hidden Agenda

If we try to create a just society
We are Stopped! By the hidden agenda.
If we raise our heads
and shout out loud

We want to be counted!

Someone, somewhere
will express their anger --
and say --
That's not fair.
So we just leave things as they are
And slowly surrender
To the Hidden Agenda.

*Roy Somerville*
*Portsmouth South CLP*

## Lady Beautiful

How came she to be sleeping rough
In silk shirt and designer jeans?
Is it that chic to be so tough?
A thrill to live below her means?

I saw her as I hurried past
The huddled masses, door by door;
Then cameras! I stand aghast
To watch her posing with the poor.

New blonde, expensive on the eye,
Here dossing where the deadbeats wine
And dressed to kill where others die
Of cold or drugs. Shop windows shine,

But sharp as her stiletto heels
Chill winds through cardboard city blow
Their grim alarm call, and it feels
As if today there'll be more snow.

But snuggling warmer in her mink
And swaying to the limousine,
She leaves cold doorways where men shrink
Into despair. The streets are mean:

And meaner still when bright guys flaunt
A model's silken warmth so near
To faces haggard, bearded, gaunt,
Where life is hopelessness and fear.

*Robin Brumby*
*Taunton CLP*

## On Overhearing a Member of the William Morris Society call the Prime Minister a Philistine (1986)

The highest goals that man may yet attain,
Who's bought his council house and is employed,
Are to get shares in Telecom and Gas
And see the Tories safely home again --
His heart is vacant and his soul is void.

*John Dearing*
*Reading West CLP*

## Market Forces

There is no selling point
In just keeping somebody's
Head above water.

Nobody wants to buy
A listening ear which will
Prevent deterioration into depression.

Only the "mad" and the "bad"
And NOT the "sad" are to be
Given valuable therapeutic time.

We were told their is no longer
Money, except for the most acute.

Yet it is more often despair
And NOT mental illness
That leads to suicide!

*Anna Corser*
*Stratford-on-Avon CLP*
*(A Mental Health Trust worker)*

## The Young Man

The Young Man was feeling exceptionally low,
He was lonely and confused with no where to go
because he had no money and was unemployed.
He'd got into debt when his savings became void.

He wasn't lazy, he had looked for work,
He'd tried at the job centre without any luck.
He'd no family no friends, he felt a misfit
He became homeless waiting for his benefit.

On the street he died of cold one mid-winter day.
They had closed down the shelter and forced him away.
So, did this person exist, how true is this story
Last year the shelter was closed, (thanks to a Tory)

*Kim Northover*
*Southampton Test CLP*

# War Story

A young recruit, A soldier soon
A mothers silent pride

A barrack square, And drills 'till noon
A war's advancing tide

A round rammed home, An order given
A screaming imp of hell

A widow's tears, A broken heart
Born of a bursting shell.

*Ben Blackman*
*Teignbridge CLP*


# Haiku For Human Rights

For A Chinese Orphan

A girl with no name
in a room prepared for death.
Unwanted gender.

For Ken Saro-Wiwa

Put Shell to your ear
hear the rush of an oil well
snap of a black neck.

For The Victims Of Racist Police

Fair skin and strong heart
protect you in battle with
long arm of the law.

For The Minister Of Prisons

In a free country
a baby's first cry is heard
above rattling chains.

*Sue Johns*
*Mitcham & Morden CLP*

## Building Bridges

Trains pass over bridges
Water flows through bridges

People huddle under bridges
Hopeless, hungry, freezing
Cold, with the winter night,
Chill, with the lack of love.
Huddled people cast away–
Unwanted garbage, disposed of.

I want to build a bridge
That will stand through time.
A bridge into the future
Where no people sleep
In rags and cardboard boxes.
A long bridge, a strong bridge,
carrying hope, and people
Into a new future.

Each of us can do something.
Each of us can be a brick
For this new bridge we need.

Will you build it with me?

*Rosemary Browning*
*Weatbury CLP*

## Land Of Make Believe

Tory, Tory, Jack-a-nory
   Tell us please a fairy story
Thou art the master of such art,
   Listen now! and we will start.

Once upon a time there was
   A handsome Prince behind a glass
No! handsome's not the word to say,
   Perhaps he was a little Grey.

His courtiers were both brave and bold
   They saved Old Folk from getting cold
They saved the needy and the sick
   (and in the process, got rich, quick)

The prince produced a people's charter
(as useful as a bridal garter)
'you will have rights' the charter said
(the right to sleep, when you're in bed)

And so the fairy story goes,
For how much longer no-one knows.
We hope our 'Hero' wins through soon
To rid our land of Gloom and Doom

*Linda Levy*
*Stevenage CLP*

## Fiadh'aich De Or'ainn
## (Song Of Anger)

The song of night is calling,
Its potent music blends
With the magic mist that's falling
On this land of northern ends.

The song of pride is weeping,
Its grieving never ends;
For land of cattle and of reaping
This land that for its people tends.

The song of hate is welling
Hate of monetary trends,
Hate of Major without telling,
Hate of all he comprehends.

The song of love is human
And where we rise or fall
Love of man and love for woman
And that love will conquer all.

From the Highlands and the Islands
Our stubborn pride is king.
Forced to forge in foreign outlands
But they can't force us not to sing.

*Macille Mhoire*
*Yeovil CLP*

## Toward Our Dreams

To end the plight of those who are in need
  To fight the power broker's lies and greed
    To claim the right to represented view
      To find true friends who'll always help us through
     To save a countryside long under threat
    To shelve those failed themes without regret
  To shape our children's future as we do
To build a brave new world where dreams come true

> *Ray Wornes*
> *StIves CLP*

## When

When we've torn down the prisons which others have built
to chain up the speakers of truth ;
when we've altered the minds of the uniformed thugs
whose clubs break the skulls of their youth ;
when we've broken the bombs and the planes and the tanks,
all the weapons with nothing to give,
and we've planted more crops in the war-ravaged fields
so that all of their children may live --

When we've all learned to see through the cunning and greed
of the masters of money and power ;
and we know that all platinum, diamonds and gold
are worth less than a rose bush in flower ;
when the poisons are gone from the earth and the seas
and no acid rain stings our eyes ,
and we've freed all our brothers and sisters at last
from the shackles of hatred and lies --

When the walls are all gone, both the ones which have guards,
and the uglier walls in our minds ;
and our eyes can begin to see clearly enough
that we know just how long we've been blind ;
may we walk hand in hand through the rivers of peace
when the dark night has turned into day ;
'til our bodies and minds become clean ;'til the blood
and the madness is all washed away.

> *Peter Hall*
> *Mid-Bedfordshire CLP*

## Don't Despair, My Friend

Do you think that I don't know
How it is to feel so low?
Just one of millions, all the same,
Slowly losing the survival game.

The clock still turns its cycle full
But time has changed, and life's so dull.
The hours stretch out beyond the day,
Or so it seems, with time to play.

Different doors open – and close.
They've seen so many I suppose.
And still like you I try some more,
Perhaps today, an open door.

*Alexia Hamilton-Morris*
*Clwyd South CLP*

## Hard Work For The Trees

Hard work for the trees
growing so majestic.

Hard work for the sun
gilding every twig distinctly.

Hard work for the river
holding that city upside down
without dropping it.

Hard work for the earth
pushing out our food.

Hard work for us
sharing it
and with those to come,
handing on the globe as we fade
without dropping it.

*Gabriel Chanan*
*Windsor CLP*

# A Northern Nursery Rhyme

*(A song, written on the closure of Swan Hunters Shipyard)*

Old King Coal was a sad old soul
And a sad old soul was he,
So he called for his pipe
And he called for his bowl
And he called for his fiddlers, three.

But the pipe had gone out
And the fiddlers had fled
And there was nothing left in the bowl,
So they wrung their hands
And shed crocodile tears,
And that was the end of King Coal.

Mary had some little lambs
Whose fleece was white as snow,
And Everywhere that Mary went
The lambs were sure to go

The rain came down
From that faraway town
And laid waste the pastures below.
Now Mary's gone
She couldn't go on
And Mary's flock no longer roams.

Once there was a beautiful Swan
Who lived by the riverside.
For a hundred years, or maybe more
He'd been part of the peoples lives.

Then the last cygnet flew,
Flew right away
To the grey of a gunmetal sky.
And the people wept
for the people knew
They were watching that old Swan die.

Post Script
Now King Coal's gone
And so has the Swan
And Mary's flock no longer roams.
We've all been conned
Right from day one
And Mary's in a private nursing home.
                              *David Chaytor*
                              *Sedgefield CLP*

## What Are You Doing To Help?

Why should pensioners suffer with no money?
Each day, brings heartache and pain.
They sit praying for better days.
Shopping at Oxfam.
Making tea and beer last for hours.
It's very sad.
With no love.
Sitting in a empty house.
Talking to walls.
Dreaming of equality
Watching their children cry, for corn
and looking for heroes.

*Kenneth Mood*
*Blaydon CLP*

## Conrad Noel and the Battle of the Flags

He hung the Red Flag up in Church
And abandoned privileged pews;
Paraded the Sacrament through the streets,
Which 39 Articles forbid one to do.

Latter day skinheads: the Kensite crew
Were fed up with this, and came to town
To teach Noel a lesson in virtue
And pull the Red Flag down.

A struggle ensued that lasted for days,
The flag was pulled down, and abused,
The National Press and H G Wells
Gave their earnest views.

In the end, a vote was cast
And the Left gained a victory;
Conrad and his Morris Men
Were preferred to Tory morality

Though the battle of Flags has long since ceased
And Conrad lies at peace,
Thaxted Church is still a shrine
For every rebel Priest.

*Stuart Snowden*
*Leicester East CLP*

## Double Standards

No family lunch today
Mum's gone to Safeways
Dad will make a sandwich
His wife now works on Sundays
Bread, four pack cans and bar codes
The way it is today.
The lawyer and the dentist
Enjoy a round or two of golf.
Lunch at three,
Then the heavy papers
Not for them to work on Sunday.
They like their weekends free.

The homeless on the streets
Hands held out for anything you offer.
Chastised for daring to beg
By Tory politicians
Who accept clandestine handouts
from foreign friends
To boost their already bulging coffers.

Waiting in the ever growing queue
Because a government does not care
His Giro to collect.
"Sorry son, we heard that you were paid
For two days work
You failed to declare".
Orders passed on by those
Who fiddle their taxes
And do bum business deals
Conveniently forgotten.
But theirs is an oversight
Of course.

Families struggle to make ends meet
Now being lectured by overweight
Double-chinned fat men in tight suits,
Who backsides hang over
An average sized seat.
"Money? You want more?
It's you who keep the country poor".

Yet still more cuts in education and health
Yet still more for the bastards to squander
Yet still they sell the nations wealth
Yet still more needed to keep that family
Who live beneath the Royal Standard
Or could it be
Their flag and ours
Are now
The flags of Double Standards?

*Sylvia Cox*
*Medway CLP*

## Lakeland Obituary

We negotiate the lower slopes
of Coniston Old Man
Contemplating the mountain
from the marsh
Freezing
to observe a heron downstream

A cheerful return
Rewarding pint in Coniston

Later we shower away hill dust
Switching on the radio
The real world
catches up with us
John Smith's death

The view of Windermere
fails to cheer
Walking into Ambleside for Chinese
The gardens full of tulips
no red roses

Drinking wine
Listening to Smithy's admirers reminisce
We share a tearful kiss.

*Sue Johns*
*Mitcham & Morden CLP*

## The Complete Man

To be a whole man, strong and real,
    To understand the common weal,
No use if you've been used to silk,
    You'll never know the poorer ilk.

To hunger, thirst, and reel with cold,
    To watch with care those near grow old
Before their time, and not complain,
    Whilst wealthy folk go by again.

But one thing they can never know,
    The love that sets you all aglow,
As never with a thought for self,
    You give your all, it's more than wealth.

*Stan Curry*
*Dover CLP*

## Unbind Your Heart

Unbind your heart from those who'd keep your mind
                        on trivial things ;
From those who are afraid to live ; who cannot laugh or sing ;
From lovers who want you to play the games that they control ;
Who do not understand your dreams, or the beauty of your soul.

Disown the ones who'd keep you from the things you need to know.
To know may hurt, but it's the kind of pain which helps you grow.
You have to get beyond their lies to find out what is real ;
You must use your own eyes to see, and your own heart to feel.

Unbind your heart from those who do not cherish our good earth;
Who know the price of everything, but not what things are worth;
Who do not care if trees stay green or if the seas stay blue,
But only for their balance sheets and the profits of the few.

Your youth and beauty stand above their ignorance and greed.
You've seen the dark decaying streets, the eyes of those in need.
Like us you long to help them in their misery and pain,
Somehow to plant the seeds today that hope can grow again.

*Peter Hall*
*Mid-Bedfordshire CLP*

## The Ballad Of Number 10

Enter Health with worried look,
Is her goose about to cook?
Then comes Law and Order Chief,
(Couldn't catch a petty thief)!
And Deputy with Lordly frown,
Thinks he should wear the Leader's crown,
But takes his seat, content to wait,
The crash inevitable as fate.

The P.M. looks around his crew,
and tells them all just what to do,
To keep their jobs, no matter what,
Despite the truths by, Richard Scott,
"Just keep me here, I'll see you through,
No matter what they say you do,
Through graft and scandal, porn and sleaze,
I'll see you're not brought to your knees.

And when it's back to Commons time,
(And mountains there we have to climb),
We'll bury truth and decent acts,
With shouts and jeers and many pacts,
At start of day we'll kneel to pray
And think of things that we should say,
To help the strong and crush the weak,
Lose jobs galore, but ours we'll keep.

And to the 'other place' we'll send,
Those who will help us in the end,
To keep the working rabble out,
(A few get in  without a doubt),
But chinless wonders ready there,
Will greet them with a glassy stare
And wave around their Eton Ties,
whilst seeking to maintain our lies.

With serious mien and steady eye,
I'll fool the mass and I'll get by,
Because the party does well know,
As confidential tricksters go,
My brazen neck and studied frown,
Will face the Opposition down
So one more bluff or two and then,
It's back for tea at Number 10.

*Stan Curry*
*Dover CLP*

## The Tory Theme

You may have had a rotten time,
House re-possessed and job on line,
But never mind, just take it all,
Whilst we up top will have a ball.

Our promises like pie crust new,
Are broken  as your hearts are too,
But through it all as sure as sin,
We'll dump it all in our waste bin.

Now quiet there, the future's fine,
Just toe the Tory party line,
Now keep quite still, don't rock the boat,
We'll lie like hell to keep your vote.

*Stan Curry*
*Dover CLP*

## Socialist Anthem

Conservatives have broken down.
Their rebels stand aside.
Friends and colleagues challenge them
And swim against the tide.
As a river floods its banks
Spreading far and wide
Socialists can celebrate round the countryside.

If building bridges left to right
Brings failure, try again.
Make fully comprehensible
Your bitterness and pain.
Faces on a stormy sea,
Waves of swaying arms.
People power benefits, domination harms.

Degrading squalor lingers still
With sickness, pain and grief.
Amid this shattered harmony
Tomorrow brings relief.
Many losers, no-one wins
Capitalist games
Children who are innocent suffer in their flames.

No branches grow from stony ground.
No economic power
Among the broken images
In Major's darkest hour.
Rising from a dream of hope
Victory is now.
Win elections everywhere. This your final vow.

*Nancy Reeves*
*Blackpool South CLP*

## Thatcher's Lot (That's Yer Lot)

*(On being made redundant in 1980)*

Maggie Thatcher Grocer's daughter,
Leading Britain into slaughter,
As Prime Minister No success,
Getting Country in a mess.
Causing classes
Among the masses,
where the rich get rich
and, there's nothing surer,
The poor get poor
and even poorer.
Redundance abundance and
Millions on the dole,
How much more
Can we Britons thole?

Let Britain get back
to rationalised planning
With Labour creating
more nationalised manning.
Get rid of the Tories
for once and be strong
and let's have a Country
we're proud to belong.

*(thole – to bear, to put up with)*

*James Barker*
*Edinburgh Central CLP*

# First Class, Post

*In gratitude for the special issue postage stamps commemorating the bicentennial year of the death of Robert Burns.*

That Bard called Burns was such a lad
 He died so young it makes me sad
To think what poems might have come
 From one with such a lucid tongue.

Its right and proper we should show
 Respect for him where e'er we go.
The postage stamps are just the trick
 We honour him with every lick

His name is not a household word
 Yet everyone his songs has heard,
Like 'Auld lang Syne' and 'course ye knows
 'My Love is like a Red Red Rose'

Then 'Sleekit Cowrin' Timrous Beastie',
 'Flow Gently Afton', that's a feastie,
Does 'Charlie he's my Darling' go
 With 'Green Grow the Rashes O'?

'Ye Banks and Braes o' Bonnie Doon'
 Is yet another Burnsie tune.
And there are many more besides
 That Scottish poet's volume hides.

There's one I like above the rest
 I think I like this one the best
Because it puts them in their place
 Those lords and such with all their grace.

The poem is the best he spoke
 For poking fun at mighty folk.
'Twas for a banquet he prepared it
 It's quite amazing how he dared it.

He says "that fellow called a Lord,
 Tho' hundreds worship at his word,
Is but a fool for a' that.
 And real folk laugh at all that".

"The rank is but the guinea's stamp,
The man's the gold for a' that."
Is quite as fine as any lines
That Shakespeare ever scrawled at.

If only he were here today
I'm sure he'd have so much to say
With every leading sleazy Tory
Our Robbie would be in his glory

So thank the Post man for his thought
And happiness that he has brought.
Perhaps my poem does the same
For you, although it's pretty tame.

*Derek Alan Taylor*
*Stafford CLP*

## BSE

See her, she has finally won freedom
Dream like from a Minister's insomnia
Turned into something nightmarish and gruesome

Safe untouched, our fear becomes a barrier
One once degraded, placed upon a platter
Now gives our lanes a likening to India

Because a daily diet of grey matter
Fed with disregard of what is natural
Has made her crazed quite mad as a hatter

See her, officially she's invisible
Speak of her in whispers
Hush the whys and hows
This soft eyed lunatic they have made terrible

Hailed taboo by holier than thous
For she is one of England's many sacred cows.

*Sue Johns*
*Mitcham & Morden CLP*

## Major Connections

John Major phoned the other day
From Downing Street. It was to say
He wanted my complicity
To ostracise the EEC.

Poor John seemed greatly overwrought
In urgent need of my support.
I said, 'The Social Chapter's right',
Put down the phone and said, 'Good-night'.

Next day he growled, 'We'll privatise
The railways. They'll reduce in size
So if you go from Waterloo
And lose your way what can you do?'

He thought Conservatives were best
So wanted me to hear the rest.
'I'll privatise the NHS
'Till patient care is less and less.

You'll never get us to create
Improvements paid for by the state.
The poor and destitute must pay
If True Blue Tories have their way.'

My boy considered it was cool
To gain a place at Public School.
Then Major asked if it was wise
Of me to turn down such a prize.

I told him I was not amused
And left the Commons feeling bruised.
A Comprehensive School is best
Where children need no written test.

John Major, I am so annoyed
At seeing all the unemployed
The private cats are getting fat.
New Labour can't approve of that.

The bank then tried to repossess
My house so I was in a mess.
I sauntered round to number ten
To ask for his advice again.

'I need a Tory candidate.'
I said, 'You must be joking, mate.
What me?' I cried, 'you must be mad.
For when you're gone we'll all be glad'.

*Nancy Reeves*
*Blackpool South CLP*

## Topical Adaptation of W H Auden's "The Night Mail"

This is the night train stuck at the border,
The privatised railways are so out of order,

Routes for the rich but none for the poor,
The break up of BR will soon become law.

Letters by train, never again
Freight on the Rail, a certain fail,
Exploited staff and resignations,
The unions banned from negotiations,
Continuation of unmanned stations,
And closing down more destinations.

New pretty faces
Take up their places,
Clad in such uniforms just to be leered at
By overweight businessmen, there to be sneered at.
Trains on the main routes to cities and towns,
Only at rush hours to rake in the pounds,
No trains for people stuck out on a limb
So travel for them is increasingly grim.
Buying a ticket for every line
From Bristol to Blackpool – how asinine.
I'm sorry its folly, it's glaring, it's wearing,
The sale and the break up and increase in faring,
Madness, stupid, bound to fail,
The trains and the network should stay British Rail.

*Bruce Nairne*
*Harrow East CLP*

### Poverty Trap

I see a band of pale-faced
And weary men all dwindled down
By days increasing in their weight.
No sustenance no dwelling place
For generosity is rare.
I watch them brooding over death
Or living still on charity.
I'm waiting for their hearts to break
As, sick in soul and body both
They pray for immortality
Because my name is Poverty.

I kneel beside an ancient crone
Who stays alive through strength of will.
She mumbles 'twixt her toothless gums
Until two icy lips are still.
As vultures glide above their prey,
I swoop on unprotected men
Who sink into oblivion
Or cease to care until they die.
They know that all their lives will be
For ever in my cunning trap
Because my name is Poverty.

Her spotless steps are scrubbed each day.
Imperfect clothes are darned and patched.
She manages to find a way
To pay her bills. I take a look
Into her eyes and see the pride
Still gleaming there, refusing help.
I know I cannot break her will
As children scamper in the dirt
Or laugh with untold happiness
Until they learn subservience
Because my name is Poverty.

*Nancy Reeves*
*Blackpool South CLP*

## Cardboard City

Labour-saving gadgetry,
created for us by
mysterious technology,
spews from factory production lines
in cardboard boxes.

Gaudy packaging always managing
to catch our eye
and shore up ramparts
of over-fed society.
Rich men throughout history
told poor men how to live
and now they give
cardboard boxes.

Each soul is a precise no-one
escaping from themselves
in dreamlike solitude.
Not for them the promised return
to more than empty boxes.

Eyes, once sharp as thorns,
are lost in mists of sorrow.
Immortality is a long word
so keep tears for tomorrow.
Like drowning rats they reach out
for their rightful freedom
from the need to stay alive
in more than cardboard boxes.

This devastated world is lonely
for only few have understood
those people striving to be good.
Are voices ever heard
to question or condemn
this mess of modern selfishness?
Have we ever thought about regress
to cardboard boxes?

*Nancy Reeves*
*Blackpool South CLP*

## The Tory MP's Lament – 1996

Back in nineteen seventy eight
The British worker took our bait,
Allowing us through Downing's Gate
  . . and working people helped us.

The power the Unions had enjoyed
Would go if they were unemployed
And they would never fill that void
  . . if working people help us.

Our dearest Margaret had her say,
The people backed her all the way.
Her Falklands venture gave her sway
  . . while working people helped us.

We saw the dole queues grow and grow.
Now that's success! – you ought to know
For that's how private profits grow
  . . as working people help us.

But Margeret's firmness brought her down
And Tory colleagues wore a frown.
Annoyance grew in every town
  . . still working people helped us.

John Major came upon the scene
His background set a whole new theme
And once again we saw our dream
  . . would working people help us?

The years went by, and things were good.
Our privatising programme stood
We'd make a killing while we could
  . . while working people helped us.

But passing time has scattered down
Banana skins upon the ground
And now it all seems so unsound
  . . can working people help us?

We know the trick, it's worked before
We tell them tax will be no more
They'll all come flocking to our door
  . . if working people help us.

We've cut so much from public dough
Yet people tell us we must go
But why on earth, I'd like to know,
  . . won't working people help us?

(Perhaps there aren't any left.)

*Derek Alan Taylor*
*Stafford CLP*

## Privatisation

This apology of a government,
     so obsolete and spent,
It's time to say 'get on your bike'
     'twould be a blessing heaven-sent.
The arrogance and the avarice
     the callousness and sleaze,
Nigh on seventeen years in office
     we've been brought to our knees.

The squandering of our Assets
     the anguish it has caused,
Trading in the market place
     they have never paused,
Stripping all of them quite bare
     conscience they have not,
Carrying on regardless
     out nation prospers not.

There's barely naught to barter now
     we're victims of their greed,
On a carousel of misery
     on which the fat cats feed,
Low pay, the dole, the homeless
     the time of reckoning's due,
The red rose will prevail
     instead of Tory blue.

*Martha Prescott*
*Scunthorpe CLP*

## Then And Now

Our Great-grandfather, William, died at 38,
Down the pit.
"An accidental fall of stone",
That's how the coroner recorded it.

Our Great-grandmother Mary died at 29 – Typhoid.

Nine children orphaned. It would have been ten,
Only Anne died of typhoid too.
Two big coffins and one little one.
No money for gravestones.

Joe was all right. He was 12 and had a job
Down the pit.
He got lodgings with another miner.
The rest went to grandparents, aunts, cousins,
Anywhere rather than the workhouse.

We can all rest easy.
Nothing like that ever happens today.
Of course not! How could it?
There aren't any coal mines left
In north-west Leicestershire.
And the water supply is reliable. In Yorkshire,
        we know that!

*Patricia Riley*
*Leeds North West CLP*

## Lost Hope

Oh how I wish I had a job to earn my daily bread,
Instead of looking downcast, then I could raise my head,
To regain my confidence which I once enjoyed
Search as I may it's fruitless for I'm still unemployed.

I've even got upon my bike, but still it was in vain.
Through sunshine and through shower I have been soaked in
                                                    rain.
Despondent and discouraged, and sick unto my soul,
I'm beginning to think that I will spend my life upon the dole!

*Martha Prescott*
*Scunthorpe CLP*

## Forest Rumblings

*In early times, England, like most of the island of Great Britain, was heavily forested, chiefly with oak and beech in the lowlands and pine and birch in the mountainous areas. Woodlands now constitute less than 4 percent of the total land area.*

In the forest something stirred –
Overhead, that mighty bird.
Have you seen the Tory vulture,
It's a part of British culture?

In the forest something whispers.
Awful rule this Prime Min-i-ster's,
With his fellow crows around him
Schemes afoot will surely ground him.

In the forest something creaked –
Vibes from havoc they have wreaked.
Money is their only pleasure –
More for them but less to treasure.

In the forest something snapped –
Forest Council's been re-capped.
Nothing now for Education
Fat cat's took it all – damnation!

In the forest something screeched –
Wheel's on train the oil's not reached.
Maintenace is not afforded,
Train sale soon will be recorded.

In the forest something died.
Makes me sad to be alive:
All the poor folk's degradation
In this shadow of a nation.

In the forest something grew –
Labour's back with something new!
Socialism's dream is living,
O'er the earth, support they're giving.
New hope now for new beginning,
'Care' and 'Fair' will keep us winning.
This time will we make amends
And show those Tories **we** have friends.

*Derek Alan Taylor*
*Stafford CLP*

## Student Loans

Dear Mr Major,
Lend me a pound.
My grant isn't big enough
To keep me I've found.

I've got no money
I can't buy books,
And my bank manager's giving me
Very funny looks.

No money for food,
I'm six stone two,
And when I stand by a light
You see right through.

I love my lectures,
My work is fine,
But at malnutrition
I draw the line.

So please Mr Major
Gi's a student loan,
Pay the gas and 'lecky off
And re-connect our phone.

*Rebecca Yoell (former student)*
*City of York CLP*


## The Just Rose

Rose you are mighty.
The invisible worm,
That arrived in the night
In the howling storm:

Has flown your wood
Of lustral dew:
His bitter descent
Does your life renew.

*Neil Jeffery*
*Mid Norfolk CLP*

## Suzi's Home

Suzi has a home: it's only four walls square
The corridor echoes but you would not say it's bare:
It's patterned with bugs and cigarette burns,
The lino trips her baby where the corner turns.
She's living in a prison, yet she's guilty of no crime;
Her sentence is unending, and she's running out of time.

The Council sent her here, said 'it won't be for long,
The hostel's very friendly, you'll soon feel you belong',
But two years have passed; it's all her son has known
Their only crimes are poverty, and wanting a home...

She's living in a prison, yet she's guilty of no crime;
Her sentence is unending, and she's running out of time.

Suzi writes letters and talks to MP's
Calls on Councillors, and makes considered pleas:
'What am I to do? What on earth have I done?
I'm locked in this prison before my life has begun?'

She's living in a prison, yet she's guilty of no crime;
Her sentence is unending, and she's running out of time.

There are no homes for you and me
Else we wait on the list till we are fifty-three;
If you've got no wealth, a home is NOT for you,
They're not building any so here's what we do:
                    ( if we're LUCKY, that is!)

We sit in a prison and were guilty of no crime
The sentence is, unending and we're running out of time!
                    (RUNNING OUT OF TIME!!)

*Debbie O'Connell*
*Runnymede & Weybridge CLP*

## Listen Out Louder

Listen out loud to what I have to say or you might miss the message between the lines. War is only destructive and no one has ever really won one, and we could all loose the last one. Instead let us fight a peace, such a peace would mean that the various factions would take part in contests, not only sporting contests, that would mean that the sporting venues would be shared between the two zones of conflict, thereby bringing in trade to those zones, also work competitions, involving armies of workers, tools and materials going into each other's countries and competing from a distance, there could be forest planting and Disney world building contests. It would be a constructive way of solving differences which would vanish, because the winners would win the issue, and the losers would win the peace.

This isn't really my idea. Who is it that said love your enemies and do good to those who curse you, yet the crazy thing about it is we crucified him for it.

*John D Leng*
*SedgefieldCLP*

## A D-Day Veteran Point Of View

I did my bit in World War two
So that you Tories could be so blue
I've come to think you hate us so
With the things you're doing to us blow by blow.
I cannot afford glasses to see you
With this dispiteous Mrs Bottomley
My teeth are sadly going to pot
I'll just have to leave them in to rot.
V.A.T on fuel, it won't affect you selfish, greedy lot
It will be me you see, I'm a few bob over the top
You Tory MP's on thousands of pounds a week
So selfish and greedy that you seek
To push us under, the mild and the meek
Profit, profit is the number one
Not for the many, but for some
Why did my comrades fall on the beaches
For you greedy selfish load of leaches

Was it for market forces and dog eat dog philosophy
Or was it for Major's classless society
Firms so often near to crash
Can legally take our pension cash
When come the time, it surely will
You will have to face your maker
What then will you have to say
I invented the Citizens Charter

*Ken Morgan*
*North Wiltshire CLP*

## The True Hypocrites

They privatised the water, telephones and gas
For speculating fat cats, their fortunes to amass
The airlines, railways, oil, electric power
Everything for human life that springs from Nature's bower
The "One Nation", strategy is still the, "Major", theme
But that has failed so, "Dirty tricks", is now the basic scheme
The Harriet Harman episode has plumbed the Tory pit
For having shown her mother love, she's now a hypocrite.

The stated Labour policy, against selective schools
And Government statistics, of young illiterate fools
Suggests that, "Comprehensives" with, "Fast track", for the bright
Must enhance our nation, and make Britons erudite
But since they grabbed utilities against the Labour vote
And put the power in private hands to have us by the throat
It means that shadow ministers will face a Tory blitz
For using their facilities, they're Labour hypocrites,

Hypocrisy has always been a part of Tory life
Their lying manifestos, the sleaze and party strife
The dirty tricks too numerous to sully voter's minds
And now the word, "Hypocrisy", with fond hope that it blinds
Their, "Machiavellian striving, to hold the reins of Power
Has no bounds of honesty, a real, right, royal shower
And like a tabby cat at bay, that hisses, claws and spits
It's centred well in voter's minds, they're Tory hypocrites.

*Bogenshutze*
*Daventry CLP*

43

## Contemporary

No matter how many lies the Right may feed
Some of us will always succeed,
We'll educate ourselves to the truths
To separate us from the fools.

A Frenchman isn't just an onion seller
And all Aussies don't wear corks,
Not all women yearn for makeup
Not all men want just sex and no more.

Britain isn't Great and democratic
But a country losing community and magic,
Our Kingdom isn't United
But class-ridden and deplored.

Look out of my window
All the little houses look the same,
A thousand different lives are locked away
With singular views and similar pains,

I don't even know the folk
Who fester feet away
Some don't even know their own neighbours
Whilst living close but miles away.

All the wonder of this world is wasted
And in some cases denied,
Things will get worse before better
Stooping low before getting high.

*Ian Synclére*
*Leicester West CLP*

## I'll Have To Ask My Husband

What then the worth of Women's Suffrage?
Far more than any man supposes.
So great the cost, so small the message,
A basic right to bread AND roses.

*Patricia Knight*
*Carlshalton & Wallington CLP*

## A Healthy Society?

Tiny Tim – let him die,
there's no cot where he can lie.

They close the Wards and fill the graves,
but life's preserved for those who pay.

There's plenty of money for a tax incentive,
so to fail the sick is financially inventive.

I've just been bitten by the bug,
making money is such an available drug.

*Malcolm Thorpe*
*Lewes CLP*

## Meat Mountain

herd up the ramp into well secured stalls
doe eyed round the arena then back again
bleating and bellowing

stark walls in cavernous halls licked with paint
to pacify bleeding hearts and make it psychologically
more pleasing to the eye

in the melee there's a mulish bray
that falls on deaf ears – he's a stubborn brute
but takes the proffered titbits sheepishly
mother hens squawk at wayward chicks

pens securely chained add to the rage
especially for left handers un-catered for as usual
well filed like lambs to slaughter
sacrificed to market forces
a numb electric buzz announces your turn
though they say it's quite humane

who will start me off
with subsistence rates
for this man's dignity
going
        going
            gone!

*Andy Terry*
*Stoke-on-Trent North CLP*

45

## Madam Chung

*(Chinese restaurant, Alderley Edge)*

Among a noisy, innocent people
In that place she had lived,
Happy to inhabit a steeple--
Like tenement of the choked city;

Till an ancient aircraft fluttered,
As a spent moth its antennae,
To waft them (the husband muttered)
To "lands of opportunity';

Now, in this quietness, she flowers;
Muses between the laying of tables;
Threatened only by English showers,
Or the ache of absent children.

*John Bateman*
*East Devon CLP*


## Could You..?

Could you beg in the streets?,
Could you stand the shame?,
Could you hold out your hand and say
"Please help me, I'm not to blame"?

Could you look into peoples eyes?,
Could you accept the looks of disgust?,
Could you withstand the threat of arrest
from the policeman you used to trust?

Could you smile when children look at you?
Could you watch when you hear them say,
"What's that person doing Mum?",
As she hurriedly drags them away?

Could you stand the freezing wind and rain?
Could you imagine feeling so low?
Could you imagine another long night in the cold,
A cardboard box your home, nowhere else to go?

Could you foresee any hope worth living for?
Could you comfort yourself and say:
"God be with me, keep me safe tonight,
Let tomorrow be a better day"?

Could you beg in the streets?
Could you still keep your dignity?
Could you look people in the eye and say,
"Vote Tory, and end up like me"?

*Martin O'Toole*
*Leominster CLP*

## Care In The Community

Homeless people on the street
  Begging at the workers' feet,
Children fled from homes too tough
  Doing drugs and living rough.
In the subways underground
  The destitute a shelter found,
Cheered a while by buskers' song
  Until we have them moved along.
Foreign tourists stand and stare
  They can't believe they're sleeping there,
But in this land of market forces
  There must be some that fail the courses.
Elsie Jones will die alone
  Evicted from the nursing home;
No-one cares she's ninety-eight
  The fact remains, her Fees were late
And poverty is just her fate
  For she's a burden on the State.
She never earned enough, you see
  To live the life of you and me.
The hospital is now a Trust,
  A pity that it's just gone bust
And terminal patients turned away
  Because the GP cannot pay
But once a month the nurse will call
  For National Health is free to all.
But after all we've all been told,
  If out-of-work, or ill or old,
'Your duty is to serve yourself,
  Stop scrounging off the Nations' wealth.'

*Patricia Knight*
*Carlshalton & Wallington CLP*

## Private Members – Public Dissemblers

'Midst anger and breast-beating the proposition was laid,
And a number of members silently prayed
That the Old Boys would still hold the majority vote
And there might just be time to scuttle the boat,
If a deal could be done when they met down the pub
To prevent a mere woman from joining the club.
So they all scurried off to plot and to plan
To keep their club pure as is right for a man;
But they lost in the end as befits double-dealing
And the women burst through the club-house glass ceiling.

*Patricia Knight*
*Carlshalton & Wallington CLP*

## Death Throes Of Public Service

Where once there was service
There now is a Vision.
The staff has been cut,
But they all have a mission.
They must focus on outputs
And identify needs
And their name-badge will ensure
They'll be judged by their deeds.
"Fix the problem," they're told,
"Not the blame."
But there's nobody left
To deal with the claim.
And Core Values defined
By the Citizens Charter
Disguise the slow death
Of the public-owned martyr
Burned at the stake
Of Tory ambition
The scapegoat of the Right
In a privatised Nation.

*Patricia Knight*
*Carlshalton & Wallington CLP*

# Our Year To Forget

*(A look back at 1992..the "annus horribilis)*

Dear Queen, I was sad when they told me that you
Had been having an "annus horribilis" too.
So I thought it might comfort your Highness to hear
That it wasn't exactly *my* favourite year.

For they chopped out my tumour –"the size of an egg";
I had jabs in my buttocks, my arm and my leg;
I had probes down my throat, and tubes up my nose,
And I learned where the end of a catheter goes.

I had masking with plaster and deep radiation,
Severe diarrhoea and acute constipation;
I took thousands of tablets, and became very knowledgy
'Bout the meanings of rude-sounding words like "oncology".

They did things I can't mention without seeming crude,
And solved my weight problem—I just stopped eating food.
For roast beef and Yorkshire can ne'er pass my lips,
And I've forgotten the flavour of sausage and chips.

When I was working I often would say:
"I wouldn't do Her job for double the pay."
Now, glandless I never will know how it feels
To attend all those banquets and eat all those meals.

So like you, I've got problems, but no use to grouse.
At least no one so far has burned down my house.
No cameras appear when I'm trying to relax,
And, as far as I know, I don't owe any tax.

So chin up, You Majesty, be of good cheer.
We're not what we were, but at least we're still here.
But one thought, I'm certain I share Ma'am, with you:
I don't want another 1992!

*Norman Ford*
*Stroud CLP*

## Ten Thousand

Ten thousand brave young soldiers
Ten thousand uniforms
Ten thousand rat-tat guns
Ten thousand neat white crosses.

Some gave their lives – for something
Some lives were snatched away
Some lives got lost somewhere, somehow.

Ten thousand children playing
Soldiers on the rec.
Ten thousand children saying
"My Dad was killed. Was yours?"
Ten thousand widows signing
Ten thousand pension books.
"Next please."

The project team is busy
Designing a better gun
To spew more bullets faster
Ten thousand in a burst.

> Bob Pinder
> Burnley CLP

## The Human Demise

The future of our race
has something bad in store
because of our technology
pollution and our war.

The human race should know the score,
see when there is a war on
the fit men go and fight.
The weaklings they stay home of course
and cowards they will always run in fright.

The human race should know the score,
technology preserves the sick
and kills fit men through war.

The human race should know the score,
extinction wont occur
completely over night,
but what with our pollution
well you never know it might.

The human race should know the score
gene degeneration
will come in geno waves
so they will have to specialise
so they will all become each others slaves.

The human race should know the score
his name is ultraspiflicus
should we become no more.

The human race should know the score.
The human race should know the score.
The human race should know the score.

*John D Leng*
*Sedgefield CLP*

## Rumblings Of A Social Conscience

Admire our ornate display
Symbol of prosperity
a semi-detached, and a car
To travel in the fast lane
But, have we thought
Of the deposed?
Those without means,
Teeming masses of humanity
Whose destination is unknown
And can there be
Serenity, and peace of mind
If we neglect
The struggles and aspirations
Of the poor
With social justice to secure
We can only tread
The path of peace
Caught up in the quest
For righteousness
Not some pious hope
But a world shared
And spared
The abuses of untrammelled power.

*Norman Mason*
*Mid-Norfolk CLP*

## A Moral Crusade

Back to Basics for the Tories
Heartened by their great P.M.
Bathed in dreams of former glories
Doughty ladies and Trusty men.

Policies of hope and fortune
From the ashes of the past,
Banish then the Opposition
Commonsense will rule at last

The Nation now must stand together
Grasp the new sobriety,
Weak and feeble to the gallows,
Embrace a new Society.

Eighteen years of Tory values
Who could say they got it wrong?
Enlightened now the Government preaches
Until another scandal comes along.

Weasel words to hide their blushes
'Silly',' foolish', perhaps 'uncouth'
Obviously too much to ask for
A Minister to tell the truth.

*Patricia Knight*
*Carlshalton & Wallington CLP*

## At The Elections.

Crack of dawn, yellow sun.
No more leaflets that's all done.
Chitter chatter in the car.
Red and yellow stickers, roses are everywhere,

Sitting getting sun tanned, sociably socialising.
Six hours sitting in the sun turn me over this sides done,
Scoring sheets at a station.
"You got a good job" is what the voters say.

Service done, a change of pace.
A snack, a sliver of savoury pie.
Tot up them numbers, tick that sheet.
People working while they eat,

Coal black boxes, red wax seals.
Only one side shows, where were the blues.
Mountains of white sorted to neat tidy mounds.
Counted checked, counted again.
Smiles and cheers at the scrutiny's culmination.
All our Labour had not been in vain.

*Dave Kane*
*North Tyneside CLP*

## The Jobseeker's Charter

Now, managing director in the newly-private sector
Would suit a man like you down to the ground.
You just punish all those shirkers, by sacking half the workers,
And raise your pay by several million pound.

Or maybe your ambition is to be a politician
A job that offers very rich rewards.
You could sharpen up your wits, spending week-ends at the Ritz,
And still have time to serve on all those boards.

Selling guns and rockets can quickly fill your pockets;
Such deals, they say, can bring in quite a sum.
Though profits come much easier if there's war in Indonesia,
And it helps to have a P.M. for a mum.

Pity you're too loyal to have –er friendship with a Royal,
"Telling all" can be a well-paid racket.
Though maybe you could hope for a bit-part in a "soap"
Their sexy tales can bring in quite a packet.

But since you're conscience-driven to earn an honest living,
For the useful. kind of toil you're here to seek,
I'm afraid there's little call; in fact, there's none at all.
Perhaps you'd better come again next week!

*Norman Ford*
*Stroud CLP*

## Labour Of Love

This deep inside anger will erupt with great force
        when election day comes very soon.

For they (I'll not mention, nor think of their name, for
        thinking's too precious to waste)

Have tried to deceive us with waffle, and piffle, and nice
        men on telly, gobbledegook, twaddle and lies.

The wool that they pull will not cover the view, that we
        have for this great nation.

The Blues must come out and so must their snout, from the
        cream troughs all over the country.

For the old and the young, the weak and the strong the waged
        and those that have nothing

Must share in this wealth and community health, must live
        out their lives and be proud.

Their interests come first in our party, New Labour is here
        so take heed.

We do not need cake, we want bread Sir, the bread of life
        will sustain us quite well.

To imagine is, but one thought away, we can create whatever
        we will.

This power is free for all thinkers, we'll make policies,
        solve problems, move mountains.

        Especially if they are blue.

*Larry West*
*Bassetlaw CLP*

## BR

The train now standing at platform one
  Is very late and not much fun
    The train now standing at platform two
    Is rather grubby and far from new.
     But gentle traveller have no fear
    A private train will soon be here
      It may be late, it won't be cheap
And there's fraud on the line in a bloody great heap.

*Bill Looker*
*Edmonton CLP*

# To The Gallant

*(on surviving 18 years of Tory rule)*

Where's the injured? Where's the sick?
Which private ward did they pick?
Where's the dying? Where's the dead?
Couldn't find an empty bed.

Where's the houses? Where's the homes?
In the street the children roam.
Where's the love and where's the care?
"The money's needed elsewhere".

Where's the witness? Where's the police
When will all this hardship cease?
Where's the Judge who views oppression
As an act of sheer aggression?

Where's the pupils? Where's the classes?
Where's the schooling for the masses?
Where's the text books? Where's the teacher?
Where do all the children feature?

Where's the young and where's the old?
Public utilities sold.
Their  homes then taken by the bank
While the fat cat bosses swank.

Where's the Steel? Where's the coal?
Here's the workers on the dole!
Where's the pride, they once would yell?
Gone, just memories to tell.

Where's the Nation? Where's the Voice?
Time to give them all a choice.
Let's once more stride down the lane
Heads high, and let's be great again.

*Neil White*
*Bolsover CLP*

# I'm All Right, Jack

Long ago I made a solemn resolution
when elected a Conservative MP,
I'd approach each proposition from the principled position
of "Precisely what is there in this for me?"

I made it clear to everyone I dealt with
I must be paid for everything I did.
If I at your suggestion ask a minister a question
it will always set you back a thousand quid.

I told a minister just how expensive
it is to keep a comfort-loving wife,
then we danced a gay fandango when he put her on a quango
and now we lead a most luxurious life.

I've seen to it my brother's doing nicely.
The hospital he runs is now a trust.
So full they fill their purses, there's no money left for nurses,
and if the patients die of it they must.

If I'm defeated at the next election
I'll suffer quite a large financial loss,
and so it's not surprising that I'm bent on privatising
some enterprise of which I'll be the boss.

The public may complain of poorer service
when I've dismissed three-quarters of the staff,
but why should I be troubled when each year my pay is doubled
and I'm the one who gets the final laugh?

*Charles Hobday*
*Kensington & Chelsea CLP*

# Curricula Vitae – Section 6 'Anything Else To Add'

Tell me not that dawn has broken,
I'll just disagree.
The night goes on. There is no ending.
No sun will shine for me.
They say there is a new day coming.
That I can't accept.

I fear the postman's 'Last Reminder' knock.
No hope. Just nothing left.
"Recovery is on the way", we're told.
Told and told again.
It's pain they say I'll suffer first,
Before the promised gain.
Don't tell me there are jobs out there.
I've tried: year on year.
Retrain. Restart. It's just a laugh.
If so, why the tear?
Chronic Depression; Samaritans; Psychiatric Care.
Sleepless nights. No Rest.
Means Testing just means not enough.
Living: itself a test.
Tell me not that dawn has broken,
Nor that dawn will break.
The night goes on. It's never ending.
Why wake for waking's sake?

*Clifford Painter*
*West Suffolk CLP*

## Rendezvous At Bob's

Christ met Lenin
At the coffee-stall
Near Peckham Rye:
Deep in debate,
Compromise? Thought I...
Could this be true?
Shared a cuppa
Like true comrades do,
Lengthy discussion
Till the morning star,
Dawn broke over those two.
As the sandled-one retired
He bade farewell to Vladimir,
Wearing shoes.

*Terrence St.John.*
*Tunbridge Wells CLP*

## Cruise Missiles

I wonder if those 'back room boys'
On far-off distant spheres,
Are blessed or cursed with sayings,
Such as 'All's well my dear'—
Do they take us seriously?
For old planet Earth must seem,
Just a tiny speck in space
Whither a myriad lights do gleam.
Inquiring minds might well ask,
'How far eternity?' or so...
And then rebuffed by the 'old wives tale'
Like 'One must never know!'
I wonder if science can lend
An ear, to those with set ideas;
Ideas like, 'God is in Our Universe'
Or, 'We Rule OK, don't fear!'
And should this planet go off its path
As a shooting star goes thither,
Perhaps some Boffin in the cosmic dust
Will record when we pulled the trigger.

*Terrence St.John.*
*Tunbridge Wells CLP*

## Lines On The NHS Cuts

I am the accident victim
Who found the casualty unit too far
I am the dialysis patient
Who needed a hospital car
I am the working-class person
Who didn't have the cash
I am the premature baby
Who couldn't take the motorway dash
We don't picket or protest
We can't do that you see
We relied on the NHS
And now we RIP

*Sue Johns*
*Mitcham & Morden CLP*

## Tatters

Darting here and everywhere,
cooker here, washer there.
That's what society offers our kin.
In pick up truck a right old knacker,
men once proud are now the tatter.

Begging here and everywhere,
principles gone we do not care.
That's what economy gives our kin.
Nothing to do our minds they batter.
Never bother become a tatter.

Steelworks closed Jobs all gone.
There is no use in carrying on.
Maggie's hammer hit and splatter,
the Oak destroyed arise Sir Tatter!

Men once proud men of steel
scour wasteland to cadge a meal.
Oh men in commons you've killed the golden goose,
but does it matter?.
NO you say, you have a choice, be a tatter.

Darting here and everywhere.
Nick some lead here, some brass there.
Reduced to criminality.
When coppers come they'll see us scatter
and live for tomorrow to be a tatter.

Oh actions vile you closed our mills and took our dignity.
A folk, once hardened men of steel, there's nothing left for
me. Our hopes are gone, our region battered,
the steel we worked is now just tattered.

*Richard Parkes*
*Dudley South CLP*

# My Town

How vibrant is my town
now they have shut the steelworks down.
Vibrant with the chorus of singing drunks who have found
solace in cheap refreshment establishments.
The desire to work and the ethic forced down by politicians
that just don't care.
The drink to stem a floodgate.

How happy is my town.
Now huge shopping centre is a Jewel in Dudley's crown.
All work goes to those that commute from elsewhere,
anywhere, our people looked down upon and only fit
to stack shelves and mop floors.
My folk skivvies to chinless wonders.

How lovely is my town, trees once lined pavements, looked
nice, then they cut them down.
Where trees once thrived, they came in the darkness of night,
not asking but sawing, chainsaw biting,
replace with concrete pots an eyesore to us all, scabby trees
and we were supposed to be grateful, their vision of
loveliness.

How decrepit is my town
as they are forced to close the quality shops down.
Parking meters in place, snarling, telling all that officials in
charge are yearning to break the back of the local trader.
Boarded windows, signs To Let, why now you see a town
upset.
Decrepit through neglect.

How healthy is my town,
they attempt to bring our spirits down. In us they have picked
upon the very instinct to fight back.
Survival of the fittest and people of Brierley Hill forged iron
to beat Hitler's bombs,
a spirit of steel which made us what we are.
Brow beaten but have not lost the war.
You'll see Staffordshire folk, proud, true, hard rise once more
not content with being labelled West Midlands.

*Richard Parkes*
*Dudley South CLP*

## Excessive Greed

'Tis sure that Hell will slowly freeze
Before we're rid of Tory sleaze.
The sea will dry and pigs will fly
When Tories cannot tell a lie.
Till fish don't feed and eunuchs breed
We'll always suffer Tory greed.
So what will make John Major act?
What dire, earthquaking, filthy fact
Will shake him off his neutral fence
And stop the Tory decadence.

Our Euro vision right off track
Leon Britton got the sack
We're opting out of vital laws
We suffer sleaze while Major snores
A Government with greed unchecked
That fritters all our self respect
The Brits who, "Never shall be slaves"
Have epitaphs upon their graves
"The land we made For hero's fit
the Tories couldn't give a spit".

For those who think what might have been
Had there not been, "Who would be queen"
When Brits still walked a worldly stage
No football yobs to rant and rage
Few cardboard boxes forming homes
Less laundered cash with Zurich gnomes
The Tories still could boast less tax
And now impose the very max
That green and pleasant land has gone
Gone with dithering Major John.

*Bogenshutze*
*Daventry CLP*

# The Ousting Of Thatcher

It's not a male prerogative,
either sex should know
That when a woman's gotta go,
a woman's gotta go.
The thought of losing Finchley
and stabs from underneath
The fusillade of arrows
and shots from Edward Heath
Many fine libations
have gurgled down the hatch
To celebrate the house of Commons
losing Mrs Thatch.

To Europe she's inimical,
the Brits have felt her spite
For any sign of sympathy,
she takes a US flight
No more the fishwife rhetoric
and suits of royal blue
No handbag swinging matriarch,
to flagellate her crew
Be sure her thirst for power,
this move will not appease
Until she leaves this mortal coil
and Britain's turmoil ease.

Elevation to the Peerage,
seems now her only chance
To bend the Lordly muted ears,
her ego to enhance
The Upper House is beckoning
and seems a likely patch
To preach the ranting gospel,
according to St Thatch
Dismay and apprehension
invade those peerless heads
E'en before her footstep,
their Hallowed cloister treads.

*Bogenshutze*
*Daventry CLP*

## Bewhiskered Dogma

You chose him with exceeding care
    And thrust him in the spotlight glare
His charismatic streak for goal
    Has caused the Tory bell to toll
But clause four reared it's ugly head
    Provoking words best left unsaid
has no one thought of Britain's lack
    Of cash to buy the assets back?

The country's assets should be ours
    Like Mother Nature's April showers
But nationalised companies can't compete
    With quangos in the driving seat
We've had our history lesson now
    Clause four is not a "Holy Cow"
Forget the dreams of yesterday
    It's teams that lose who err and stray.

Dissenters want to rule by rote
    But first we have to win the vote
With sixteen years of Tory rule
    Now's not the time to play the fool
Don't ape the Tory disarray
    Unite and know we'll win the day
If clause four is your firm intent
    You'll never be in Government

*Bogenshutze*
*Daventry CLP*

## I Believe In Labour

I believe that every child should have every opportunity
Pensioners every comfort,
Every criminal should get punishment without impunity
Sufferers every treatment sought.

I believe that every worker should be given every chance
I believe everyone should take a political stance
And that the Tories have danced their last dance.

*Edward McCabe*
*Dover CLP*

## The Opening Gambit

Sovereign's escort, golden coach,
full panoply of state
The Queen swept into Parliament
to read the nation's fate.
Such waste of money, prodigal,
no sparing of expense
To read a speech so lacking
in tact and common sense.
No remedial statutes
or turning from the course.
John Major has an abject fear,
another stalking horse.

The main event is imminent,
the budget in the offing,
Champagne by the bucketful
the fat cats will be quaffing.
Talk of tax cuts in the air
to salve the backbench hearts,
No help for institutions
or cash to save St Bart's.
A tax cut is the Tory ploy
to gather voters quick
But if we fall for that again
they've sold the five card trick.

To pay for Tory tax cuts
more pillaging and loot,
Hospitals, single mums
and schools will feel the boot.
To make the right wing happy
is now the Major thought,
With good deeds on the starboard side
the helm is hard aport.
Is it any wonder
that those for country dare
To chuck the Tories overboard
and vote for Tony Blair.

*Bogenshutze*
*Daventry CLP*

# To The Ubiquitous Sycophant
*or Zenith To Nadir*

When peoples of the western world went overboard for oil
'Twas love of gold not stratagem they pumped from Arab soil
They little recked home fuel neglect would take its dreadful toll
Nor yet the dust blacked human mole who mines our native coal
The fact that foreign speculators run our offshore rigs
Will not ensure that Britain has the power to shoot down Migs
So when will British subjects learn that those who drum up strife
Number not within their ranks the toiler and his wife
But greedy power hungry men who've always kept it rife
..............The British Ruling Class.


When lust for gold suffused the minds of oil exploiting men
The sword they still considered then as mightier than the pen
The halcyon days of British might massed wealth for several score
Successive Tory governments gave nothing to the poor
Small wonder that the Empire whose subjects gave us power
Seceded from the parent stem when patriots struck the hour
When average British citizens can well and truly think
Of all the aristocracy who've brought us to the brink
These men have no true blue blood nor yet a common link
..............The British Ruling Class.


Our native sons poured out their blood to give the country wealth
In foreign swamps and torrid heat they fought and lost their health
Sons of the sea all British born, yet pressed to fight the foe
Who cares what they suffered for it was so long ago
Successive generations have fought to keep the grip
On dominions and colonies whose allegiance seemed to slip
Whose hand was on the leash when we slipped the dogs of war
Whose hands are stained with so much blood from Britain's
                                               richest store
And who if they're allowed to – will do the same once more
..............The British Ruling Class.

*Bogenshutze*
*Daventry CLP*

## Lest We Forget

I lost a limb fighting a strategic rearguard action,
C.O. said, 'the free will respond with an ever grateful reaction'.

But the energy bills today I cannot pay,
and the winter ills strike like 'battle death chills'

'Alas, no extra money for old age', the P.M. says
and the market must not be careless.
then why do so many indulge in such a way
that I wish I could *afford* to be 'legless'.

*Malcolm Thorpe*
*Lewes CLP*

## Not Just Nostalgia

"Socialism is dead" declared
the balding fifty-something
Man
in the tweed jacket.
The Others
nodded in Agreement, their heads
bobbing up and down like
Driftwood in the ocean.
He nudged her
Violated
Body with his riding boot
and surveyed the Deep Crimson Stains
that looked like
Rose petals on her White dress.
There,
in all her Stillness,
she defied his pale blue eyes
To Love Her.
And he remembered
a young girl whose picture
he used to
keep
in his wallet a long,
Long
Time ago.....

*Sabrina Doyle*
*Brent East CLP*

## On Yer Bike!

Life's despondent when your on the dole.
'you're a lazy git', so I've been told.

Some papers imply I act like a tramp,
even though my hand has writer's cramp.

The industry where I live needs vital resurrection,
but the economy compass points in the wrong direction.

Our house is worth 'nothing' it cannot be sold,
to buy 'down there' I need a pot of gold!

And my family and friends are heaven sent,
I will not leave them for an extra cent.

*Malcolm Thorpe*
*Lewes CLP*


## Rotten Cores.

The shadows lengthen on the grass,
An apple drops from nearby tree.
Night soon will fall and time will pass
With darkness and lonely reverie.
The cool green apple in my hand
Is blushed with pink-- as if ashamed
That greedy grub's devoured it's core
And no-one wants it anymore.
THE WORLD HAS CHANGED
It's core is rotten, we can see
Just like the apple from my tree.
We pollute the air, dump nuclear waste,
And warring nations get a taste
For violence -- and many lives are lost
Let us now pause and count the cost.
Poverty, greed and corruption now abound,
Care and compassion are seldom found.
Better values we should strive to keep
Or future generations will have cause to weep.

*Mona Majerski*
*Wellingborough CLP*

## Waiting for the End (After William Empson)

Waiting for the end, chaps, trying to buck the trend,
What can I or Kenneth do?
What's to become of me or you?
Haven't we kept faith, true blue,
Huddled still together, chaps, waiting for the end?

Shall I attack the sleaze, chaps, knowing it will tend
Certainly to displease, chaps, waiting for the end,
Firms we need to please, chaps, where we can find a friend,
Causing party funds to freeze, chaps, waiting for the end?

Shall we rely on lies, chaps, trying always to pretend
It's the truth Murdoch supplies, chaps, waiting for the end?
Knighthood's a well-earned prize, chaps, for those who don't offend
While self-sacrifice a peerage buys, chaps, waiting for the end.

Shall we smear a Euro-sceptic, chaps, waiting for the end?
Teddy Taylor, so apoplectic, chaps, waiting for the end?
Wouldn't life be much less hectic, chaps, would I lose a friend,
And I'd be less dyspeptic, chaps, waiting for the end.

Shall we butter up the Prods, chaps, hoping things will mend,
Though they're alike as peas in pods, chaps, waiting for the end,
All cantankerous sods, chaps, determined never to unbend,
Blindly serving private Gods, chaps, waiting for the end?

Shall I give way to Hezza, chaps, who could that offend?
My wisdom teeth can't be deferred, chaps, waiting for the end,
Shortly to return, I give my word, chaps, the Party to defend,
And not a Tory heart unstirred, chaps, waiting for the end?

Shall we run for glory, chaps, tax cuts and spend, spend, spend?
For country, Queen, and self 'Vote Tory!' chaps, waiting for the end,
And should defeat be gory, chaps, and from office we descend
The City will take care of us, no panic, chaps, waiting for the end.

*Patrick Sayles*
*Shrewsbury and Atcham CLP*

## The Lord Mayor's Banquet

It's the glitter of the crystal and the shining of the silver
On the gleaming white damask on the tables;
It's the shimmer of the silks and the dazzle of the diamonds
On the gorgeous gowns.
And I'm troubled by the contrast of the lavish wealth displayed
here
And the hopelessness and need behind the  high-rise broken
windows on the dark side of the town.

*Mary Naylor (Aged 70)*
*Bridgwater CLP*


## Tories Today

The men from Eton, Harrow too,
From playing fields to Waterloo,
    Have always laid their claim to fame,
    By playing fair, to play the game.

That was in days of long ago,
When Britain did her best to show,
    That British men, for all to see,
    Were best by far, on land and sea,

But now they're hard, and tough and bent
Goodwill to you is only lent,
    And when it's time to pay your bills,
    You'll find they're hard-to-swallow pills,

We'll have your jobs and houses too,
We'll lend you cash and then we'll sue
    When you get sick and old and bent,
    You'll think the grave was heaven sent,

When time to vote is drawing near,
We'll knock a penny off your beer,
    We'll ease a little on the yolk,
    That bears upon you simple folk,

And maybe then you'll think again,
That we are those with right to reign,
    Our blood that's blue sets us apart,
    And never mind we've lost our heart.

*Stan Curry*
*Dover CLP*

# A Tory's Lament

I remember the last time that Labour was in
Said the Tory MP with a smirk,
There were power outs and strikes -- discontent everywhere
And nobody wanted to work.
Taxes were high for the rich and the privileged
With workers demanding more pay,
It was all so unfair to the company boss
Whose profits diminished each day.


But we got back in power and we showed them what's what
By tackling those union mobs.
This wasn't too hard as the companies closed
And the workers were left with no jobs.
We never forgot all those strikes in the pits
Determined to get our own back.
We closed them all down then bought coal from abroad
And gave thousands of miners the sack.


We privatised everything -- nothing was safe
Electricity, water and gas.
Some workers bought shares and then voted for us
Each one hoping to make lots of brass.
Then next came our plan for the great NHS
To dismantle it all was our aim,
With fundholding doctors and hospital trusts
"It's safe in our hands" was our claim


Don't pay rent on your home was the message we gave
Take out a big mortgage instead
Trot off to the bank -- get a loan for a car
With the Tories you're moving ahead
It wasn't our fault when the house prices dropped
Or that people were thrown on the street
Some must have been greedy and borrowed too much
And that's when they started to bleat

Folk are joining New Labour in droves every week
That's something I can't comprehend.
Don't they know unemployment is falling,
The recession has come to an end.
We've got short-term contracts and jobs with low pay,
They're better than no jobs at all,
And people work harder with fear in their hearts,
Security makes them walk tall.

I know we've left patients on trolleys for hours
Cut hospital beds year on year
Put fat cats in charge to get waiting lists down
But the people have nothing to fear
We're the one nation party – let no-one forget
We care for the old and the sick
But try as we might to get our message across
The voters still give us some stick.

So what is the lesson to be learned from this tale
As to why it went so very sour.
It's no good pretending we're popular now
When we're only just clinging to power.
The lesson is simple – New Labour take note
That a party in power for years
Takes dogma too far, whilst ignoring it's fans,
And it generally ends up in tears.

*Jill Horobin*
*Derby North CLP*

### Turning Swords Into Ploughs

All those who make a living building weapons
whatever be their colour creed or nation
whether they be shareholders or workers,
should be crippled by vigorous taxation.
That tax money along with any other
that the world allows
should be paid to those who make a living
turning swords into ploughs.

*John D Leng*
*Sedgefield CLP*

## A Rosy Dawn

Just what are we fighting for?
Why are we so keen?
Reflecting on past triumphs
Or what might have been?

The homeless sitting all forlorn
On city streets they freeze;
While Fat Cats smirk and pass them by.
Millions made by sleaze.

The ill in pain on waiting lists.
No one seems to care.
Fifteen years of Tory rule
Yields anguish and despair.

We know there is a better way.
Give people back their pride!
New solutions, resolutions,
Labour has not died.

Hope for men to plan their lives,
To work, not draw the dole.
Helping women take the lead,
A more decisive role.

Comfort for the older folk,
Who fought to keep us free.
Life chances for the young ones,
Our greatest legacy.

A different generation
Can see the human need
For democracy and fairer shares
Not based on glut or greed.

We clearly have a vision
Of futures bright and new:
Forward-looking, rosy-tinted,
Not dismal shades of blue.

*Therese Irving*
*Wallasey CLP*

## Stilton Hunts

Princess Anne
Barbados tan
Hits an anti-blood sports fan
Captain Mark
Left in the dark
Sits waiting in the car park
The Stilton Huntsman's bugle sounds
They're coming on in leaps and bounds
Driven on by the stick he wields
I show them my tail and fox-trot over the fields
Another chase
Another race
To find another hiding place
Sunday should be
Completely free
From strenuous activity
I think I should
Get to the wood
Before my game pursuers could
My route is planned
I know the land
I think I've got the upper hand
Escape route took
Me through a brook
I turn round for a better look
The dogs were meant
To lose the scent
Instead they've found out where I went
Don't expect me
To climb a tree
So that's exactly where I'll be
The dogs are vexed
They look perplexed
I jump from one tree to the next
The Stilton Huntsman's bugle sounds
To call off the bewildered hounds
Princess Anne comes into sight
She looks a bit pale, I'd hate to see her tan go white.

*Mike Pullin*
*Leicester South CLP*

73

## Ode To A Government

In times like these
the Government doth squeeze
the working man hard
making him part
with the little he has
to help the Fat Cats
that sit in high places
and pull funny faces
whilst 'Sitting' in the House
supposedly catching the 'Honourable Mouse',
they sit nodding off
while others do quaff
large quantities of gin
the women sit prim
and preen their speeches
then in the House resort to 'screeches'
we watch them in awe
not sure that we saw
the Rt. Hon Gent on the right
pick his nose with delight
the Speaker nods 'yes'
and announces the next ass
who stands up tall
and pretends to know all
then waffles away
the same as yesterday
and the day before that
and the day before that
we put these men here
we elected them fair
but what have they done for the man in the street
who find himself short, and really can't make ends meet
they give you more cash
then take it back in a tax
how can we survive to make Britain Great
when all they can do is moan and berate
any foolish soul who wants to work hard
to make this land's future, and find a new bard.
We'll gladly toil from morn to night
if we thought in time that it might

make this country and us that live here
happy and fruitful, these burdens we'll bear
if only the government gave us good reason
to not turn away and think of treason.
Make all that live here swear allegiance to the Flag
then there will be nothing to 'gag'
we'll all be ONE country we'll all be ONE race
AND NO-ONE NEED BE AFRAID OF SHOWING THEIR FACE
be it black or white
WE WILL ALL BE ALL RIGHT

*Lin Manning*
*Huddersfield CLP*

## Voice of the Unemployed

Some believe God loves them –
Lucky so to think.
Some trace
A Pattern in Life's Carpet –
Their lot to be
A grimy warp-thread –
Part of the pattern yet.

> The uninvolved, the fortunate,
> Look on and preach
> Old facile platitudes,
> Bitter to the ear:
> "There's work for those who want it."
> They deplore
> The "work-shy and the layabouts", those who
> "Think the world owes them a living."

Still my eyes are clear –
Reactolite – or none of it –
I know myself to be
The grubby scum, washed up at the wave's edge,
Gutter-stale orange-peel the sweeper missed,
Grey dirt on hospital walls, beyond the cleaner's reach.

> Look from a bus on swirling crowds below;
> We are become as dust indeed –
> Expendable, waste-products, detritus.

*Jean Cardy*
*Croydon South CLP*

## The Memory

My father came home from World War One
To live in a "Peace" which had just begun,
But his wounded knee did take its toll
And lo! my dad was on the dole.

He was a man who knew the right
That people have to make a fight,
And use their voices with their vote
To build a life of worth, and note.

I, his son, in World War Two
With others, knew just what to do
To bring alive Democracy
And this we did – it's plain to see.

Fraternity, Equality
Through many struggles civilly,
Is what we really did produce
Protecting people from abuse.

Work now for a party which knows what to do
To bring back our dream, alive and anew.
"Fair play for all" should be our call,
And abolish forever the fear of the dole.

*Sidney Warren*
*Greenwich & Woolwich CLP*

## The Boss

He was keen, he was mean, he was smart, he was cool,
    One of the new managerial school;
At ease with statistics, a chart or a plan,
    Though never at home with a flesh-and-blood man.

He won praise from head office, never stepped out of line,
    With reports and accounts always rendered on time.
From questioning orders he always fought shy,
    And espoused every cause handed down from on high.

He'd few ideas of his own, but he talked a great deal
    In that meaningless jargon, designed to conceal;
Words of one syllable seldom would do,
    And he never used one word where he could use two.

He read no books, heard no music, never had any fun.
  At the mention of culture he reached for his gun.
He didn't collect stamps or make things out of wood,
  But gave his career all the time that he could.

He succeeded in life, I suppose you could say;
  His empire expanded, along with his pay.
When he left, no one mourned, no one echoed his fame;
  For friends he had none – I've forgotten his name.

*Norman Ford*
*Stroud CLP*

## Defeating The Tyrants

Those damnable Tories, they've closed all the pits.
  They're pulling our health service slowly to bits.
With Tories in power of one thing I am sure,
  The rich grow still richer, the poor remain poor.
We don't ask for much, just the  basic man's right,
  But for each thing we need, we have always to fight
The Tories are laughing they're happy you see,
  For they're making a fortune from you and from me,
They do not go hungry they do not go cold.
  They're making provisions for when they grow old.
But what of the homeless, the old and the poor?
  Do Tories give a damn? No, they don't I am sure.
They just care for the rich man, they like his applause,
  They tell him 'scratch our backs and we will scratch
yours!'
So brothers and sisters I'm sure you must see
  We must throw out the Tories and set ourselves free.
We must all stand united and make them take flight,
  Only then will we see all that's dark become light.
We must care for ourselves, as has always been so,
  We must confront the Tories and tell them to go.
We want what is ours, our own piece of the cake,
  For the sake of our children and their children's sake.

*Glynis Cooper*
*Bolsover CLP*

## A Cockney Lament

John Major
Don't want to know
That the wards are closing
'Cos there ain't enough dough.

The Government, he says,
Throws in masses of cash
Whilst the doctors conspire
For the sake of a bash.

Major pleads patience
For the absence of beds
Though aware before long
The poor sods will drop dead!

*Jack Moss*
*Hendon CLP*

## Homeless

My mother always used to say,
   "You'll be a great big man, one day,
You'll have to mind your P's ad Q's;
   Be not too headstrong in your views,
Be kind to ladies; chivalrous.
   Give them your seat when on the bus,

If only she could see me now,
   She'd really give me such a row,
A cardboard box is my home these days.
   Sickness, no job, no money to raise,
I'm glad my poor old mum can't see me,
   So down and out and very seedy.

Thoughts of the future make me shiver;
   I think I'll just jump in the river,
But then I'd meet my Mum again
   And how on earth could I explain?

*Denys Kendall*
*Warwick and Leamington CLP*

## Middle Englanders

The "Middle Englanders" who still vote Tory
   Should open up their eyes and then they'd see
There is no glory or "posh" status there
   Just jobs for the boys and greed that does not care
For the needy, disabled, unemployed and old
   And homeless people sleeping in the cold.

When people rise and labour comes to power
   Then this indeed will be our finest hour.
We'll build new homes, invest in industry
   And give all people back their dignity,
Their pride, their right to work and only then
   We'll start to build a new Jerusalem.

*Olive Wallis*
*Canterbury CLP*

# When Children Ask:

When children ask:
        Are there
        Too many rich,
        Too many poor?
        Are you sure?
                "Yes!"

        Are there
        Not enough homes,
        Not enough trees?
        Polluted Seas?
                "Yes!"

        Are there
        Too many orphans?
        Too many blacks
        Breaking their backs?
                "Yes!"

        Are there
        Too many crooks?
        Too many cars?
        Too many wars?
                "Yes!"

Can't we change it?
        "One day – maybe
        But shall we go now
        and watch TV?"
                "Yes!"

*Ilse Challis*
*Leominster CLP*

## The School Inspection

Ofsted has hit and run. The Head closes the door.
All lessons have been evaluated – good, sound and poor.
On a desk in the office forms pile up by the score –
Assessment and attainment lists, data to explore.

The school has its league position, every pupil has a set,
The teachers have been graded, every target has been met.
Slick to deliver; mark, record, assess.
Here's a 'good' for Mathematics, for Art and English less.

But what of love, faith and happiness, – beauty, self-esteem,
A joke with a friend, or aspiring to a dream?
– And the one vital lesson every child should learn –
That there's much more to life than the money that you earn!

*Peter Palmer*
*Stafford CLP*

## Reflections

Not long ago, the bells
Had rung, their advent
Songs had filled the air,
And all the usual carols
Sung, throughout
The Western hemisphere...
But now the Xmas Cards
Are gone, and all dispersed
Those happy things,
Like holly, mistletoe,
Lantern-lights, candlesticks,
And silver rings.
For is it too soon
To mention here,
That mere mortal man
In his abode,
Surrounds himself in gimmickry,
As a substitute for truth
And humanity.

*Terrence St. John*
*Tunbridge Wells CLP*

## To An Unknown War Poet.

The press ask we in khaki for a war poet and we have none.
Perhaps the conscript lacks the spirit for the deed, they reply?
But we millions know that they are wrong.
Tell us first, truthfully, the purpose of our sacrifice; no lies.
Please, not just for Britain's fame and glory; the right to be free!

Is the lot of our fathers after their battle to be ours?
Are we tools for a purpose, discarded when the job's done
Or are we proud men with other purpose in life?
Are the promises of our leaders again to be as dust?
What proof, other than mere words, of the new era to come?

True liberty we seek, and such ideals hope to attain,
Not to be bound by the shackles of the system past.
Ours is a new world where unity brings equality without pain,
To remove from all the fear of poverty and war at last.
Something, then, to write poetry, to render in loud acclaim.

*Lawrence Marson.*
*Nottingham North CLP*

## Vote Labour

Election time is here again,
Please use your vote, don't just complain
And grumble how your country's run.
Put someone in who'll get things done.

If you once again vote Tory
It will be the same old story
No jobs, less schools, more cuts until
There'll be no NHS when you're ill.
No unions to fight your claim,
(If ever you're in work again).
No longer will we have cheap fares,
Unless we get someone who cares.

So let Major be an also ran
And vote for your local LABOUR man.

*Gwen Colpus*
*Doncaster Central CLP*

## Ode To Democracy (Lamented)

What price democracy?
Ten pence off this week.
We've thrown the paddles overboard
And we're heading up the creek.

We'll talk of family values
And cover up our sleaze.
I never even met the girl –
What cheek! Next question please?

Your granny needs a doctor?
Well, that's just her hard luck.
We'll kick away her walking stick,
We don't want no lame ducks.

You've got to pay your mortgage,
Or your kids need books to read?
But Cedric wants a new Roller,
And his is the greater need.

We've sold the family silver
For a load of gawd knows what.
But come the next election,
We'll hope that you've forgot.

A little tax-bribe just in time
That should do the trick.
The electorate wont question it,
They're all too bleedin' thick.

We'll sell arms to whom we damn well like
It's profit after all.
And if asked about it later,
"Sorry – cant recall".

And if we look like getting caught
"Its the Security of the State".
Freedom and democracy?
Sorry – sold out, mate.

*Susanne Atherton*
*Telford CLP*

## UB40

Is this your first application?
Do you suffer constipation?
Have you lost an arm or leg?
Aren't you just ashamed to beg?
      answer yes or no.
Are you now a Swedenborgian?
Can you play the piano accordion?
Was your dad from Afghanistan?
Do you have a pension plan?
      answer yes or no.
We haven't any vacancies left
perhaps you ought to practise theft
estimate your credit-rating.
Ever thought of emigrating?
      answer –
We do have schemes that pay no wages,
fill in the other forty pages.

Was your auntie Cantonese?
Does your dog have many fleas?
If your mother's name was Flo
How come you're so bloody slow?

You really are a worthless swine
Try again another time.
We cannot spend all day on you,
You're holding up a massive queue.

           *Bill Looker*
           *Hendon CLP*

## The Agenda

"Come, bleed with me a year or twain",
The blessed Margaret shared her dream.
"It will be worth the pangs, the pain,
To watch the sour milk turn to cream."

And thus it was – or so 't did seem,
As Howe gave way to Lawson's boom,
A dead sheep to a lusty ram.

But after eighteen years of shame,
'Tis clear that after all the Dame
Was just a dreamer, daft as Blake,
And poor, sad England's stony broke.

*John Dearing*
*Reading West CLP*


## Elegy Of The Unemployed

*The Useless hours*

Month after month, day after day, night after night
The clocks are ticking the useless hours away.
Our knowledge grows less of what's wrong and what's right
As we live in a world filled with deceit and decay.

My grandfather said to my father:
"Work hard, study hard, and you will get a good job".
He did. He plodded and struggled and eventually went
right to the top,
He had a house, he had two cars, holidays abroad
– he was not short of a bob.
Then – the recession came – no more sales – redundancy –
everything came to a stop.

My father said to me:
"Work hard, study hard and maybe, well maybe you will get a job".
"Father," I laughed, "I have not believed fairy tales since I was six,
But if you know a supermarket where stealing is easy
or even a nice bank I could rob?,
To escape his rage I went upstairs and gave myself a Heroin-fix.

We dream: A new Messiah, a wise man from Mars,
an alien from outer space will arrive
And will treat us to new equipment.
Perhaps a gun with a magic spray,
To change our attitudes, our priorities
our whole way of life, so that we can survive.
In the meantime we wait and stare at the clocks, ticking the
useless hours away.

*Ilse Challis*
*Leominster CLP*

## The Doctor And The Manager

*(After 'The Walrus and The Carpenter' by Lewis Carroll)*

The Clarke was shining on the box,
    Shining with all his might
Doing his very best to put
    The NHS aright.
An this was odd because his White
    Paper was mostly white.

The Cook was smiling cheekily
    Because he thought the Clarke
Had dropped a monstrous clanger and
    Was whistling in the dark.
"He'll wish he never started this"
    Was Robin's curt remark.

The words were wet as wet could be,
    The plans were dry as dry.
He could not see the snags, although
    The snags were ten miles high.
No beds were promised for the sick,
    There were no beds to buy.

The Doctor and the Manager
    Were listening close at hand,
Doing their best to comprehend
    What Kenneth Clarke had planned.
"If only you were cleared away",
    Each said, "It would be grand!"

"If sevens PROs with seven slides
    Showed them for half a year,
Do you suppose," the doctor said,
    "That they could make it clear?"
"I doubt it," said the manager,
    But made a sort of sneer.

"O patients, come and sign with us",
    The doctor did beseech.
"A pleasant suite, with pleasant seats
    And magazines in reach.
And if you've got a pain, my dears,
    We'll find a pill for each."

The eldest patient looked at him
And shook his heavy head,
Meaning to say his chronic pains
Confined him to his bed.
And in another month or so
He'd probably be dead.

But four young patients hurried up,
All eager to compete:
Their shoes were brushed, their trousers striped,
Their 'Times' was folded neat --
But this was odd, because, you know,
They had no ills to treat.

Then four old patients trundled up,
And yet another four,
With wheelchairs and with walking frames
They struggled through the door
"You don't come here", the doctor said,
"We can't afford the poor!"

The doctor and the manager
Waited a year or so,
Then settled on a budget set
Conveniently low,
While all the ailing patients stood
And waited in a row.

"The time has come", the doctor said,
"To talk of many things,
Of opting out and auditors
And roundabouts and swings,
And where the cheapest kidneys are,
And whether beds have springs."

"But wait a mo'," the patients said,
"Before you say your bit,
For some of us are out of mind,
And none of us are fit!"
"No comments!" said the manager,
"Or I will serve a writ!"

"A bioscope," the doctor said
   "Is what we chiefly need.
Computers next, and after that
   A Porsche will do for speed.
So if you're ready, patients dear,
   Our trade begins indeed."

"But not with us," the patients said,
   Turning a little blue,
"After our taxes that would be
   A dismal thing to do."
"The price is right," the doctor said,
   "So kindly form a queue."

"I weep for you," the doctor said,
   "I deeply sympathise."
With sobs and tears he sorted out
   Cheques of the largest size,
Holding his pocket calculator
   To his streaming eyes.

"It seems a shame," the doctor said,
   "To play them such a trick,
After they heard young Kenneth Clarke
   Whose phrases sound so slick.
The manager said nothing but,
   "What makes you think they're thick?"

"Now, patients," said the manager,
   "Our hospital's begun.
Shall we be booking you a bed?"
   But answer came there none.
And this was scarcely odd, because
   They'd priced them out, each one.

*Gavin Ross*
*Hitchin & Harpenden CLP*

*Notes: The Tory NHS changes were introduce by Kenneth Clarke and opposed by Robin Cook in 1989. GP doctors were to be given budgets which they could spend as they saw fit, and some doctors started to turn away patients likely to require expensive treatment. The Tories could not find a direct way of privatising the NHS but the right wing think tank recommended that if they started with a managed 'market' it would not be so difficult to complete the privatisation later.*

## Party Meeting

A motion on our Branch agenda lies.
We move it, shake it, brush away the flies,
Examine it to see that it is sound,
Amend it, try to turn the wording round:

"We call upon the Party, at some date
Or other, if so minded, to create
A Socialist Economy, to do
Away with unemployment, and taboo
All wealth and war and poverty!"
That's it!

We vote. It's passed, nem. con. We've done our bit!

*Gavin Ross*
*Hitchin & Harpenden CLP*

## Indictment Of The English Voter

How could you do that my fellow countrymen?
Ignore the sobbing of a child
Not see a youngster living wild,
The weeping of a couple who have lost their home,
Ignored the generations yet to come,
See institutions great destroyed,
In which the sick who should have benefited
Left to their fate.
Pretend the idle youngsters on the street
Had somewhere else to go.
How could you, without thought
Betray your own
It's something I will never know.
I cannot understand
How by your hand you crushed
those workers like yourselves.
Took all their gains and made them all a loss.

You did it on election day
By where you put your cross.

*Marian Flanders*
*Newport West CLP*

## Maggie Roberts

*(A Cautionary Tale, after Hilaire Belloc)*

When Maggie served in Father's store,
The little children who were poor
Came in and begged for buns or honey,
For they had very little money.
"You have not brought enough," she said,
"To buy our smallest loaf of bread.
But wait a bit, your coins will do
To buy a catapult or two,
And these small knives are very good
For mugging, if you're short of food!"

As soon as Maggie stepped outside,
Six gleaming pointed knives she spied.
"No, no!" she cried, "Now don't you see,
You're not supposed to threaten me!"

Too late! Her cries remained unheard.
I dare not state what next occurred.

*Gavin Ross*
*Hitchin & Harpenden CLP*

Notes: *This followed a report that Mrs Thatcher had refused to increase Food Aid,
but pointed out that Britain was doing good trade in exports of arms to the Third
World. Shortly afterwards the Argentines used British-made weapons against our
forces in the Falklands.*

## Echo On A General Election

Sweet Echo! Say to what should I this day devote?
To vote!
But how? And how to know if truth be what they tell ye?
Watch telly!
But telly bores me. All those programmes me depress.
Read the Press!
The Press? But are they fair to all in what they write?
They're Right!
The Lady Blue, meseems she rewrites History.
Ee, y're right, she's Tory!
The freckled Welshman doth her evil creed belabour.
He'd be Labour!

The vague one says he is from both extremes dissenter.
      The Centre!
But there's a doctor saying he'll some day return.
      David Owen!
With those who wish to save the Earth I am agreeing.
      A Green!
Thank you, sweet Echo, now I shall go right across.
      Write a cross!
Oh, Echo, now you are a naughty mocker, I see.
      Democracy!

*Gavin Ross*
*Hitchin & Harpenden CLP*

*Notes: The Echo verse is an old form involving the most elaborate possible puns on the last few words. It usually takes the form of question and answer.*

## Elegy On The Myth Of The Mag God

*A poem on the career of Lady Thatcher.*

Young Grantham Mag, a grocer's girl
      Had grosser aims in life:
With "Denis, I'll make history!"
      Became his Tory wife.

As Education minister
      A mini-stir she bore
As down school drains she poured the milk.
      Next she would milk the poor.

The Iron Lady laid her eye
      On Welfare: "Well, farewell
The Nanny State inanity!
      Self-owners phones I'll sell."

Her plus, attacks on miner's strikes,
      Her minus poll, the Tax.
And so Dame Luck became lame duck,
      Hacked down by party hacks.

Twixt Henley Man and Manly Hen
      In ballot one, she won,
But not outright, and so right out
      The deed indeed was done.

*Gavin Ross*
*Hitchin & Harpenden CLP*

*Notes: The original was by Oliver Goldsmith. Henley Man was Michael Heseltine. The form was made more popular by Thomas Hood.*

## Tony Benn's Poem

My name is Tony Benn, – you know, the one that keeps a diary.
The Chesterfield electors seem to like my speeches fiery,
My socialist credentials and my common-sense suggestions,
I'm the terror of the Tory press, the star of 'Any Questions?'.

Now when I meet a quangocrat I have a set procedure,
A simple five-point questionnaire:
One, who is it agreed you?
Two, who is it you represent?
Three, what is it they bid of you?
Four, how much do they pay you?
Five, and how can we get rid of you?

If I had been Prime Minister, my first one hundred days
Would have changed the face of Britain in a thousand different
ways:
No House of Lords, a state-owned bank, the poor freed from
despair,
But such is life, I raise my pipe – Good luck to Tony Blair!

*Gavin Ross*
*Hitchin & Harpenden CLP*

## Water

Water still flows freely
As do the wind and Rain
Seasons come and seasons go
For which we ain't been pay'n

Natural, commodities
Air and water and fire
Now we have to pay for all
Services cut back to the wire

Social destruction
Nearer every day
Arrest the power from these jokers
And let common sense prevail.

*Richard Greene*
*Slough CLP*

## John Major ... Who's That?

Who's that looking through the window
Who's that knocking at the door?
It's your Tory party candidate
Begging for your vote once more.

Why does he stand there smiling
How can he be so bold,
When we pay so much for services
And all our assets sold?

Who's that talking on the tele
Telling all those lies
While a child waits on a trolley
And another patient dies?

Who's that living in the country
Hunting harmless foxes,
While homes are repossessed
And youngsters live in boxes?

Who's that wining and dining
With fat cats from the city,
While the old are poor and cold?
Does he have no shame or pity?

How can he represent you
With consultancies galore?
While he gets even richer
Your more skint than before.

Now when he calls round this time
Just tell him what he can do.
He's very sweet till he wins his seat
And then it's to hell with you.

So if you want a fair society
And government that care,
Then give this lot the elbow
AND VOTE FOR TONY BLAIR.

*Ethel Barford*
*Clwyd South West CLP*

## Unpopular Song : 1985

*At the time of the Miner's strike the author was active on the Cannock Coalfield*
*with the Lea Hall and Littleton Collieries support group.*

Now MPs talk of "Unity" and of the "Rule of Law"
Yet every striking miner knows they're what a union's for.
The Tories they know naught of us in spite of all they blab
      And we won't work for coppers
      and we'd sooner bleed than scab.

Maxwell's brays sound bonny, Lord Mathews' and Murdoch's too.
Bray asses to asses "Kiss Thatcher's ass
                    and money's there for you."
They all draw big wages for little less than gab,
      But we won't work for coppers
      And we'd sooner bleed than scab.

Thatcher's gutting out our village,and then to yours she'll turn
And even if your nose is clean no amnesty you'll earn.
She'll drive you down the railroad with policemen in the cab
      But we won't work for coppers
      And we'd sooner bleed than scab.

You know, my working brother, they've taken half our dole.
You know, my working brother, they've taken half your soul.
Remember, working brother, when their pay cheque you grab
      You're working for their coppers
      And we'd sooner bleed than scab.

Eat bread my working brother – both sides thickly buttered
To find those crumbs of comfort every Judas ever uttered,
But the vicars know who's whining and how a comrade's kiss
                    can stab,
      And they don't work for coppers
      And their Leader didn't scab.

When Peter Walker, Thatcher and McGregor go to hell
McGahey, Scargill, Skinner, Benn may stand outside as well,
But no devil's going to drive them in with joke and jibe and jab
      For they won't cross a picket line
      And they'd sooner bleed than scab.

And you can say the Unions have all gone to the bad
And take the boss's offer, and be a boss's lad;
Tell everyone your wife and kids cannot stand the tensions
Or take your premature retirements and sit upon your pensions;
Tell your son how your scabbing kept your job through the strike
But if he is looking for one, then he'd best get on his bike.
You can do what they all tell you on Telly and in the press
And be brainwashed into thinking Thatcher does things for the best;
That Britons still rule Britain and Reagan's far away,
And that Russian tanks will rumble down Wigan Pier one day;
That you've not destroyed the Union and cut your brother's throat
To buy your Spanish holiday and wife's new winter coat;
That Tory toads all love you and not one is overjoyed
To see fifty thousand of you join the unemployed.
Your money makes your world go round – your little life less drab,
   And you deserve to work for coppers
   And stay a rotten scab.

*John Gregory*
*Horsham CLP*

## Choice

Choice is brilliant!
Lets all shout it!
Choice is freedom,
Cheer about it.
Or is it that we're being led
up the garden path instead?

Green or blue,
Coffee or tea,
Now that's a proper choice to me.
But Schools and Healthcare are not the same–
Good or bad's a different game.
Choosing then is Hobson's choice.
Is that a reason to rejoice?

Choice is brilliant?
Think about it.
Choice is freedom?
I somehow doubt it.

*Jackie Harvey*
*Ilford North CLP*

## Spiral Of Despair

A middle-aged man, skilful at his trade,
Given his cards and severance money paid,
Set out at once to find another post
Wrote letters of enquiry by the host.
He searched the pages of the local press
And even tried for jobs which paid much less.
    He filled in applications by the score,
    Made 'phone-calls, knocked on doors and much,
    much more.
    Job Centres, Enterprise and MSC;
    He tried them all but it was not to be.

        Urged by his wife, he set out 'on his bike'
        To learn another trade he thought he'd like.
        He finished all the training, won applause
        For effort and time-keeping on each course.
        Reports said he was keen and should do well,
        So he came home to pass another spell
        In writing, 'phoning, sending in CV's,
        His letters desperate now, pathetic pleas.

            He changed his Rover for a Nissan 'Cherry',
            To make one Christmas just a little merry.
            As time went by he swapped this for a Ford;
            At last a bike was all he could afford.

        Soon the problem got to be much worse,
        For though in time the state would reimburse
        Money for interviews he must attend,
        He'd nothing in his bank account to spend
        To travel all the distances involved
        And this conundrum could not be resolved.

The vicious spiral downwards speeded up;
Despair and misery now filled his cup.
Once more he tried to re-extend his loan
But now the answer came, serious in tone:
The payments must be made, the debt must lessen
Or else the bank consider repossession.

To pay the bills they cut down light and heat
And covered windows up with plastic sheet.
To some degree this helped keep out the cold
But sadly, it encouraged damp and mould.
Finally all the furniture was spoiled
And all attempts to keep their home were foiled.

Housed by the Council in a high-rise flat,
This once-proud tradesman by his window sat
Watching the lucky few hurry to work
While all around him, seen through gloom and murk
Were others like him, trapped in poverty;
Through no fault of their own their destiny
To suffer an existence with no hope,

No future for their children and no scope
To exercise their talents and begin
Small businesses with which they might just win
A way out, an escape from living hell,
Perhaps in time to join those doing well.

Those were the ones whose selfishness and greed
Helped them to overlook the ones in need
And vote continuance of the status quo.
Little they cared; as little wished to know
About three million souls without employ;
To know too much might sour all the joy
They got from owning homes and cars and shares,
From foreign holidays and their au pairs.

But round the inner-city high-rise block
The figures in the adverts seemed to mock
Flaunting their comfort, property and wealth;
And feelings of resentment grow by stealth.
Eventually, somehow, a change must come;
Sadly, it will be far too late for some.

The man climbs on his balcony rail, looks round
Then casts himself off – falls towards the ground.
His wife jumps with him, so he'll not be missed–
Just two more numbers taken off a list.

*Sheila Leese*
*Stafford CLP*

## A Cautionary Tale

It's been 18 years and with things getting worse
We need to be rid of the Conservative curse
They have lined their pockets and feathered their nests
It's me, me, me and forget all the rest
All that we owned has been put up for sale
When will it sink in, this cautionary tale.
Wards in our hospitals are gathering dust
"We don't need them now that we are a Trust!"
How can we best look after those who are ill
When the first consideration is "How much is the bill".
Our schools are a shambles -- all is just not well
So many are leaving them not able to read write and spell
Even those with qualifications cannot get a job
In desperation some are driven to beg steal and rob
So many have no values and don't know right from wrong
We are all becoming weary, its been going on so long
So help us get elected a Government that will care
We're on our way, we're almost there
           -- New Labour and Tony Blair.

*Susan Campbell*
*Hitchin &Harpenden CLP*

## Care In The Community

Care in the community means sleeping in the street
    Care in the community means blisters on the feet
Who are these people who really do not care
    That the vulnerable and weak have to live out there?
When it's wintry and cold and our fires are burning bright
    We must stop to think of their terrible plight
These people need our help but, of course, that takes cash
    And the Tories would rather turn them out like trash
Some on drink, some on drugs and some are mentally ill
    They get so very little help – a very bitter pill
This system does not work – the Tories turn their backs
    No care in the community would be nearer to the facts.

*Susan Campbell*
*Hitchin &Harpenden CLP*

# Bradypod

*(The three toed sloth)*

Our leading Bradypod plodding, flaccid,
His mundane doctrine powerless, passive.
Trailing depression and inertia
Following the same destructive dogma.

Once our industries were energetic,
Now they stagnate, lie there, apathetic.
Ṣupine paralysis now lives there,
Nobody moving, and nobody cares.

Bradypod only seems to move and speak.
His inactivity is seen as weak,
Is anarchy then to be our hard bed?
Without a leader we cannot be led.

*Madge Gilbey*
*Wolverhampton CLP*


## Anthem For Doomed Youth (After Wilfred Owen)

What church bells ring for dying fields?
Only the monstrous roar of the cars.
Only the tractor engines' rabid rattle,
To flatten out their endless horizon.

No butterflies in fields, nor birds nor flowers;
Nor any sound except the striking hours,
The thrill of being driven by combined machines;
And accountants calling for their mad desires.

What poison fumes to seed them all?
Not by hands, but in their sightless eyes,
Shall shine the hell of inward sighs.
The mutant children shall be their pall,
Their flowers the plastic of demented minds,
And every desk a drawing up of profit.

*D A Clapp*
*Horsham CLP*

## The Millennium

We are hopefully emerging from the shadows and the gloom
Which have engulfed us for far too long.
With a vision of a new era of justice and peace
We must fulfil the yearnings of the people.
Co-operation, interaction and compassion must be our watch words.
The muffled protests of the homeless, destitute and hopeless
remain unheard.
Impoverished by greed of the grandiose few,
Their stunted, hollow-eyed children wait in vain for the trickle
down from on high,
Their precious lives squandered on a human scrap heap.
The elderly sick and their progeny are punished for the crime
of longevity.
Clogging up the system they are made to forfeit nest eggs for
a few months care.
These poor folk have struggled through decades of poverty,
War-time trauma, rationing and enforced frugality.
The integrity, wisdom and tenacity of our leaders
Must be harnessed to restore our fragmented society.
With Faith, Hope and Charity
may New Labour usher in the Millennium.

*Mrs Joan E Bongilli (aged 76)*
*Stratford-on-Avon CLP*

## After The Battle

*(KNIGHTSBRIDGE where an indecisive battle took place in 1941)*

I passed that way months later
And khamseen-parched brewed up.
Then idly sauntered over
To where a burnt-out tank
Lay sweltering in the sun.

I raised the turret cover
And saw what once was man.
Whose eye-less sockets stared at me.
Whose taut and shrivelled lips
Beseeched me speak to him.

His bleached white fingers
Lay still upon the wheel
His chalky toes pressed yet
Upon a rusting pedal.
A half-charred uniform
Bright once with gold insignia
No longer told his regiment or rank.

Amid the silent sound of battle,
I asked him face to face,
Just where in sunny Italy
He first saw sunshine play,
Then, what he was fighting for?

The wind blew rustling sand
Across those shrivelled lips
Which sought to murmur painfully
An answer I could only guess.

*Bob Pinder*
*Burnley CLP*

## No Solution

Can the blue eyed boy be innocent
When a lie is writ as truth
Can Caucasian hearts melt like snow
In a furnace fuelled by hate
Is it right that widows choke
On a tear gas history
And that grief is cruelly fanned
By white hypocrisy

How can blue eyed men avert their gaze
From a burning hell on earth
Why do racist brains stoke the flames
Of the shameful holocaust
Can't a heart just love a heart
in this lonely world we share
Can't the question of all time
Be why, for who and where?

*Stephen John Singh-Toor*
*St Alban's CLP*

## Cold Spell

From the north a cold wind came,
A frost lay hard upon the ground.
A wicked witch was all to blame,
And people shivered all around.

Her heart it was a frozen hell.
Chuckling at her loathsome game,
She mumbled out her coldest spell,
As the land she set to tame.

They clustered round their dying fires,
Those that had a place to dwell.
No man deserves when he retires,
Such a barren, frigid, cell.

Not a penny would she treat,
to warm their crumbling byres.
Instead she cried "Accept defeat".
Only the rich may have desires.

Just to prove she had no soul,
Three and a half million on the street,
Without so much as a lump of coal.
All seeking a way to earn some heat.

But at last she had a cause to grin,
A corpse they found, within a hole.
Not a man – so dead and thin,
But one more less to claim the dole.

Soon the cold became a sea,
Her acolyte kept warm on gin.
Drinks all round? – Not she.
The poor were left to freeze in sin.

She gave not one pathetic sigh,
But rubbed her hands in glee,
When the old began to die.
That wicked witch from North Finchlea.

*Iain A Rose*
*Brighton Pavilion CLP*

## The Difficult Art Of Management

Downsize the workforce, pay the others less,
Lengthen hours, cut breaks – pocket the excess.
A land fit for heroes, the marketeer's dream –
The poor get abuse – fat cats the cream.

Cash targets, cost-cutting, profit & loss,
Part-time for the workers – share options for the boss.
Pay late, beat the scroungers, maximise return.
Every person has a price. – You are what you earn.

*Peter Palmer*
*Stafford CLP*

## Privatis-Nation

Privatisation suits all the nation,
At least , so the Tories do say.
But privatisation  may close down your station
If railways must go that way.

In excess of inflation
You pay for a ration
Of water that's  flowing away
The directors all know
That shareholders will glow
When on higher profits they prey.

And what of poor Sid?
Remember his bid
For a share in the new corporation?
His job went in the bin
So he had to give in,
The City bought his shares with elation.

The Council house he'd bought
It all counted for nought
When the bank on his mortgage foreclosed
So he rued that fine notion of privatisation
His Tory-like views all erased.

*David Hill*
*West Suffolk CLP*

## Who Is My Neighbour

Who is your neighbour you comfortable man
As you pass by on the other side?
"Homeless and hungry" the young lad's cry
Does it mean nothing to you who pass by?

"2p off the Income Tax, that's what we want
I've made my own way in the world by myself,
A lot of hard work with some help from the wife
That is the way to make something of life.

Lazy and feckless they're always the same
Most of them only themselves have to blame".
"Come and change places just for one night:
Hard pavements, cold winds, would teach you my plight"

"I'm willing to work if a job was on hand
They need an address and so I am banned.
A house or a flat forbidden to me –
No cash for deposit is catch 23"

"My dog stays beside me, he is my best friend
His warmth cuddled close to me, on that I depend
The Salvation Army appears with some soup,
Begging and handouts are all of my hope"

Who is your neighbour, you comfortable man?
As you pass on this cold, freezing night
"Homeless and hungry" is the young person's cry
Does it mean nothing to you who pass by?

*Rosemary Banks*
*Mansfield CLP*

## The Destruction Of The "Coal Fields"

Can you sleep at nights Heseltine?
Can you sleep while 6,000 men are unemployed?
Can you sleep at nights while children say
"Mummy don't starve yourself, lets share it"
When bread is short?

Can you sleep with the knowledge that
You shut all the pits and promised
The money to set up new jobs
Knowing you lied in your teeth?

Can you sleep in your wealth, security, comfort
While 26 men a week contemplate suicide
In their despair.

Can you rest in your lovely garden knowing
That Derbyshire is ripped apart by greedy
Money-makers, scraping the coal from the living
Land and spoiling our beautiful country?

With the children  at school with their inhalers,
The schools with their shortage of books
And their crumbling walls?
Can you live untroubled with your millions
In your noble mansion's walls?

*Rosemary Banks*
*Mansfield CLP*

## Major Disaster

They lost their 'Feel-good factor'
With Tory hopes pinned round it
The thing that really riles them is
The Labour Party's found it.

*John Gregory*
*Horsham CLP*

## Alyn & Deeside

*a pensioner's milestones*

Born in the twenties, when money was tight
By the time of your manhood, you went off to fight
"A War to end all Wars!", that's what they said
To a "Home fit for Heroes" that's why you bled.

Then home to a country that soon forgot.
Poor wages – no housing, that was your lot.
Then in came Attlee and a party that cared
And the Welfare state where we all shared
Good health, good schooling not just for the few,
There seemed no limits to what we could do.

And then we came to the Thatcher years
It can only be likened to a Vale of Tears
Industries that once were our pride
Just closed down and virtually died.

The "Sale of the Century" then began
All part of the Tory wondrous plan
To privatise anything that they could
Although it was built with our sweat and blood
Health we were told was "Safe in our Hands"
But we all knew that they had other plans.

And so we come to the present day
And the Tory party still holding sway
And here you are after all these years
Of working and striving, just full of fears
Will you be able to pay your way?
Can you do without heat just one more day?
If you get sick will your home be sold?
All this isn't what we were told
A "Home fit for Heroes" that's what they said
In a Tory Britain your better off dead.

*Nina Wallace*
*Alyn & Deeside CLP*

## No Such Thing As Society

Social workers, teachers, nurses and the poor–
Poor bloody infantry in the inner city war.
Blamed for all ills, bullied and driven by fear
While their leaders blame each other, safe in the rear.

*Peter Palmer*
*Stafford CLP*

## Beautiful World

O happy lovers, so gay and carefree!
The moon shines down and what does it see?
Two happy hearts, looking ahead
To that wonderful day when they can be wed,

And live in their Beautiful World

O happy mother, with her babe on her knee!
Stars twinkle above and what do they see?
A heart full of hope that her children may see
A land of peace and prosperity,

And may live in this Beautiful World.

O happy children who play in the sun,
In fields of daisies where the rabbits run!
The songbirds sing high up in the trees,
And the clear cool rivers run down to the seas.

Enjoy your Beautiful World.

O foolish mortals, where can you be?
Looking down now there is nothing to see!
No fields of corn.
No stately tree.
Where are the songbirds? They no longer call,
No more creatures, great or small.

They have gone with your Beautiful World.

*Gwen Colpus*
*Doncaster Central CLP*

## Economics

Fancy,
    If you go to Scotland
    You can buy milk that comes from Devon
    All those miles through the traffic
    Batting along in the dark on the motorway.
    Its nonsense

Crazy,
    If you go to buy cheese
    That's made in an English farmhouse
    You will find it scarce
    The milk quota limits the farmer
    While Supermarket "mousetrap" goes to intervention.
    It's tasteless.

Savage,
    If you travel round Europe
    No longer are beasts reared locally
    To eat as decent, honest meat.
    But find brutality in abattoirs after heartless journeys
    And six-day calves deformed in tiny crates.
    It's outrageous.

Tragic,
    If you go to India
    You can find babies being bottle-fed
    On milk that came from Europe
    just think how many cows it needs
    To make the formula that gets Indians
    As allergic and neurotic as Europeans.
    It's obscene

                        *Barbara Carver*
                        *Newark CLP*

## Land Of Hope....

*Thoughts on the Last Night of the Proms*

Land of dope and Tory
Mother of all yobs
The old, the sick, the disabled
"Just spongers" say yuppie snobs.

The brave, who once fought Hitler,
Now often in poor health,
Are simply too expensive,
They're sapping the rich of wealth.

Furthermore, they witness
The land they once kept free
Through crime, rank greed and "Meedya"
Fall prey to fascist fee.

Where's the hope and glory
In a post-industrial age?
Serving junk – euphemistically "Fast Food",
For less than a minimum wage?

It'll take enormous vision,
Not promises and soft soap,
Forget the blasted glory
I'll settle for some hope!

*Barbara Carver*
*Newark CLP*

## A Sonnet On Tobacco Smoking

A plant that poisons men and beasts alike,
Called "Nicotine" and thereby grown – world wide
Despite a growers threat "great care be exercised"
Since La Medici "cure for feet" mankind has vied
To shred Tobacco, and to soil his lungs,
Because Columbus took his dreams to Spain,
Whilst savage Indians, on their bonfires flung
Leaves of "the nightshade", premier cause of pain!
Pain aimed to slay this white-man, newly come,
Sowing the seeds of hate, in Indian tribes,
Thus to be stung and slain, like human scum,
An ancient story, passed by mouth, not scribes;
So, then, our young are led to smoke, to die,
From this old plot, I beg fresh youth to fly.

*Sylvia Dixon Ward*
*Dulwich & West Norwood CLP*

## For Our Future

I well recall
The League of Youth,
heated heartfelt debate,
hikes across visionary moors,
Red Flag, a marching
tune of glory.
Young Comrades.

Heckling Tory platforms
on street corners.
Eating fish and chip suppers
from greasy, Tory press.
Taunting True Blue neighbours
on the way back home.
Fervent Young Comrades.

Here was hope for our future.
Until, like an invisible cloak,
insidiously, they settled:
the class-ridden years
of chill, pale homelessness,
Haves and have-nots.
Not-so-young Comrades.

Privatise the planet,
Shanghai the very elements
for the florid fat-cats.
Your living and your dying
at a premium,
or endure long hours on corridors.
Dead or alive Comrades.

From Tolpuddle,
Through Jarrow,
Past miners under horses' hooves.
Holding banners of proud defiance,
Still striving for justice,
Until we prevail.
All the Comrades.
                    *Dorothy Banks*
                    *Blackley CLP*

## The Falklands

War – War – unheralded War
Who thought our "Guards" could surge again
Who knew we still could wipe the floor
With Fascist troops and missile plane?
"The premier army of the World"
The media state? whilst sailors fought
On white-hot decks, (as black smoke swirled)
To save one tortured face, agony caught
In blast and flame – excruciating pain.......
Transferred to every humble home
By gift of film; thus each can claim
To see the horrors of this warring norm
Can all that wealth of future fish and oil
Ease such scars, of youth, we spoil?

*Sylvia Dixon Ward*
*Dulwich & West Norwood CLP*

## ???Guess Who???

When asked if he condemned the bomb
He deviously, but with great aplomb
said NO!
If you don't condemn you must condone
With expressionless face he did intone
NO!
It makes you wonder who pulls the strings
The IRA? He denies such things.
"We regret the loss of life".
Such empty words from men of strife.
What the hell do they care?
If they did they'd surely spare
A thought for the families in despair.

When loved ones – innocent victims – DIE
If life doesn't count
And death doesn't matter
Why bother at all
Just let the peace shatter....

*Anne Nicholls*
*Birmingham Hodge Hill CLP*

## A Vision For The Future

New Labour, old values, a Socialist dream,
Opening doors of experience, rebuilding self-esteem.
Warming hearts and minds chilled by the market creed;
Restoring soul to Government, banishing sleaze and greed.

Freedom for everyone to look, listen and roam;
To enjoy a fulfilling life in a comfortable family home.
To break down human barriers, widen opportunity and choice,
For hopes and aspirations, giving every citizen a voice.

The smile on a child's face, the caress of a breeze,
Wild flowers in a meadow, a kind word that can please.
Silence of falling snow on a grey December day.
Laughter and chatter of children in the countryside at play.

A Cantona pass, Ryan Giggs in full flight,
The flash of a kingfisher – a blur of blue light.
The touch of a loved hand, a familiar refrain.
A kind bedside word that eases harsh pain.

Vision, beauty, emotion – politics with a smile,
The joy of human contact that makes living worthwhile.
With this Socialist vision New Britain can take wings.
New Labour, and New Heart – for some of my favourite things.

*Peter Palmer*
*Stafford CLP*

## The Esther M

It's a museum!
Who'd have thought you'd see the day –
a museum.
Entry's free, that's the same.

They've Deputies kists*, hard hats,
hoggers*, pitmen's lamps.
"Display only, Do Not Touch"

> *     *kist - tool box*
> *hoggers  - mole-skin shorts*

Visitors come in summer clothes
fresh from Volvos, BMW's,
no night shift, fore shift,
shifting gear day.

No broken heads, broken backs
or owners' broken promises.
No pit ponies, only pictures
in the Esther M.

*Helen Heslop*
*Wansbeck CLP*

## Cardboard Boxes

Useful things -- cardboard boxes,

for storing shoe polish,
brushes, dusters.
Replacing glass in shed windows.

Practical for pruning privet,
functional -- temporary beds
for puppies, with a bit of blanket.

Depositories - cardboard boxes,
for children's toys - or children
who turn them into fire engines,
milk floats, space-ships, building blocks.

That was in the old days.

Now they're mobile homes - cardboard boxes!

In doorways, alleys, under bridges.
Not just one or two,
but hundreds,
like in Brazil or Peru.

Poppycock? If only that were true.

Useful things - cardboard boxes.

*Helen Heslop,*
*Wansbeck CLP*

# No Present Like The Time

We're all livin' in a land where no-one cares,
You don't get on the bus if you haven't the fare.
We're all runnin' after somethin', but we don't know what,
An' we don't give a damn for the things we got.
An' I say:

> Give me a little of your day
> An' I'll give a little of mine.
> No time like the present,
> No present like the time.

There's an old man livin' at the end of the lane,
Since the neighbours left it hasn't been the same.
No-one comes to visit him any more,
Only ghosts of the past knockin' on his door.
An' he says:

> Give me a little of your day...

There's a young girl livin' in a top-floor flat
With no lover, just the baby an' a small black cat.
She's cryin' for the things that she'll never own,
An' she feels like a leper 'cause she's all alone.
An' she says:

> Give me a little of your day...

There's a couple that I know, livin' on the dole,
An' I've seen what it does to them, body an' soul.
If you haven't got a job then you don't exist,
You're just another of the numbers on the work-shy list.

> Give me a little of your day
> An' I'll give a little of mine.
> No time like the present,
> No present like the time.

*Andy Wood*
*Wirral South CLP*

## Prattle Of A Simple Man

I used to live in a council flat
But Mrs. T. took care of that
By giving me the right to buy
My little mansion in the sky.
As a home owner I'm better than you
So now I'm a Tory blue.

Once I worked on a production line
Then I'm told the boss's job is mine
No longer am I one of the boys
Now its time for executive toys,
Look down my nose at the working slave
As I'm a Tory brave.

Everything's great – but then oh strewth!
Mortgage rates go through the roof.
In arrears then re-possessed,
My chin sinks down to my chest,
But things will improve of that I'll bet
For I'm a Tory wet.

It's off to work but the firm's closed down
So I visit job centre in the town.
Nothing there for a man of my creed
To meet my wants or even my need.
Now't to do each day 'cept play darts and pool
'Cos I'm a Tory fool.

And now I see where I went wrong
Trusting the Tories to make us strong,
So I'm going to start anew
And take a different point of view,
But as if to prove I'm still a prat
I've just become a Liberal Democrat!

*Gerry Edmands*
*East Devon CLP*

## B is for Beirut and Benwell

Apart from one close shave
near Vickers-Armstrong
Hitler never touched this place.

Avenues, pubs, community,
survived the war intact.

No war now, no enemy at the gate.

The wrecked graffitied streets,
like a set from Nineteen Eighty Four,
is home made, created by no-hope souls

Thatcher's Tyneside legacy,
who thieve, vandalise,
destroy because it's there,
an area once normal.
*Helen Heslop,*
*Wansbeck CLP*


## Song Of The First-Time Buyer

'Superior Dwellings,' the Agents cry,
'Just right for first-time buyers!'
But could we afford to meet the bills
That buying a 'Dwelling' requires?

Are 'Superior Dwellings' what we want?
Is 'Prestige' the thing we long for?
Or do we just want two up, two down;
A place we'd pay a song for?

Somewhere simple, with walls and doors,
Rooms that we'd feel right in;
A roof to keep the water out,
Windows to let the light in.

What we'd like to see 'develop',
This plan put into action:
'Inferior' homes for those for whom
'Prestige' has no attraction.
*Fred Finney*
*City of York CLP*

## Yorkshire Summer

*An incident during the Miner's strike in 1984. Two farm workers are audience to a struggle between the police (mounties) and the mass picket when a bus arrives carrying blacklegs, 'with curtains' to hide their faces.*

"Warm 'un again Tom", "Aye"
"Di yuh think many ul show?"
"They reckon so, They reckon so."
Ah took a look at the plaace he marked
Tho early on the stains o' sweat were thear.
On tunic and shot
Christ it's 'ot, Christ it's 'ot!

Graate groups o' men moved forad
An 'ell of a lot did cum
Shove and blor, Shove and blor.
Mucky mouths wi mucky dust inside um.
To and fro, To and fro.
Eh' up – 'osses!

A bos wi cottens came along
Un mounties made a screen of flesh t'aid it
Fine beasts in bloody cockpit.
Didn't seem reet, didn't seem reet!
Daft buggers jarred apart; blue thear, boys here
Sticks down, dust down, tea up, tea up!

All reet Tom, let's get to wok
land's waitin for us
Reet here on top
This harvests nearly in
Theirs is just beginning, just beginning.

*Neville Frohock*
*Lincoln CLP*

## Tarzan's Bungle in the Jungle

Small businesses are folding
So , to cure their ills,
Heseltine's proposing
Postponing paying bills.

*John Gregory*
*Horsham CLP*

## Conference 95.

The Labour conference 95
Was the best there's ever been,
Enough to turn the truest blue
A bright new shade of green.....
Sincerity was the hallmark,
Unity....the thread,
Conviction shone in every word
That every speaker said.
While the press were sat like dunces
In the corner of the room
And commentators did their best
To paint their scenes of gloom.
But nothing could detract
From what all are now debating
That this dazzling shadow cabinet
Is the government in waiting.
For it's time to put the country first,
(Before the party line),
Too long it's been the feeding trough
For selfish, greedy swine....
Still...the faithful must go home now
With a ringing in their ears,
Not only from John Prescott
But a million hopeful cheers
That have witnessed here this week
A rehearsal for the day
When we will watch with glowing pride
New Labour on it's way.

*Anthony Hilton*
*Altrincham and Sale West CLP*

## Untitled

Don't let the Tories, (back) in the kitchen
Their recipes make such a rotten mess
It may be fun to make a pun, of old school dinners
But the Tories serve frustration and distress

Don't fall, for all the cheap and tasty starters
There's a costly, unpalatable main course in reserve
And the things the Tories say, aren't on the menu
Are still contrived and cooked up slowly to be served

Look how they fattened-up, a herd of national assets
See how the work force, has rapidly declined
The Tories had a cheek to sell the people out
The cookie had to crumble – people are not blind

And the fat Tory cats, never feed on scraps
They're found hanging round the kitchen
Adept at learning recipes by heart
They know which ones to have a lick in

It's the Tories, turned the clock back
Because they have no forward plan
And now preoccupied, with personal survival
They've finally scraped the bottom of the pan

*Graham Miller*
*Torfaen CLP*

## Housing In The Nineties

How can there be so many lives messed
    People humiliated and their houses repossessed
So many people through no fault of their own
    Turned into the street and out of their home
For those who are "lucky" – one scruffy room
    Or a high rise flat and plenty of gloom
The houses they need have been sold on the cheap
    And no more built – it just makes you weep
We will always need houses at a reasonable rent
    Local councils provide that – but now they are spent
Housing associations with rents that are higher
    Profit for fat cats, with the poor in the mire
Lots who have managed to hold their home together
    Owe so much more than they are worth
                and are at the end of their tether,
Negative equity – such a burden to bear
    Their lives are being ruined, it really is not fair
Lenders gave eagerly to all who walked in
    You were considered a failure if you weren't buying
It's all been a shambles – the end of a dream
    The Tories "You must be a homeowner" scheme
*Susan Campbell*
*Hitchin & Harpenden CLP*

## Back To Basics

Some time ago we were led to believe,
    Back to basics would help to relieve
Some of the pressure from social wrongs,
    To bring some peace for which all long.

But still people sleep in doorways and such.
    A cardboard box makes a nice little hutch!
The old are still cold, not able to afford,
    The basic heating, since prices soared.

The sick can't meet the cost of their pills,
    Where the items add up like grocery bills.
Some can't take a bath, because of the price
    Of the water, now shareholders demand a fat slice.

If you're under the weather and needing an op,
    And under-privileged, you won't reach the top
Of the waiting list – priced on retail lines.
    Appendix, if you note, are up near the wines,

Gall bladders and heart ops are down by the spices.
    Today's special offers are off surgeon's slices!
The mentally ill are sent out in the cold,
    The hospice they lived in, has now been sold.

Who cares if they do a murder or two,
    So long as it's no one you know, or even you!!
We need policies based on caring foundations,
    To build a future on sounder formations.

The RED ROSE now blooming has that care
    Under its new leader, Tony Blair.
The principal being, THAT THE POWER OF ALL
    IS USED FOR THE GOOD OF EACH, if you recall.
Let us try soon for a major change.
    We could be pleased with this exchange.

*Norman Cook*
*Solihull CLP*

# Mr. Major's List.

Dear Santa,

Although I am Prime Minister there are some things I need
And I'd appreciate it if you got them here at speed.

One...a railway network, (The best the public owns),
To peddle in the market-place just like the gas and phones,

Number two is not for me, (so you see I can be fair),
I'd like my charisma by-pass to be given Tony Blair,

Number three concerns my wife, to the voters she is drab,
Give me Dolly Parton! (a double-act would be fab),

Four...to that John Prescott, (you know the one who rants),
A dose of itching powder down his underpants.

Number five, a magic rubber, Oh life would be a breeze,
I'd rub away, night and day, my party's tack and sleaze.....

If you will tick this little list, benefits abound.....
I'd open doors for Santa Clause, how does 'Sir Santa', sound.

But if you cannot manage Mighty Murdock will instead
And he'll also run some head-lines on why
                                        Santa Clause wears red.

And then I'll privatise Christmas, VAT on magic sacks,
Duty on all woolly beards..... a hefty reindeer tax.

For I need these special presents, (not the usual party tricks),
Right now please Santa Clause if I'm to win in 96.

*Anthony Hilton*
*Altrincham and Sale West CLP*


## Heads or Tails You Lose

The Tories promise faithfully
That they'll do nothing rash ;
Lowering taxes only when
The rich are strapped for cash.

*John Gregory*
*Horsham CLP*

## A Likelihood Of Flowers – A Political Allegory

It began with a death, as such things will.
And the last note, sounded over the bier,
the last long call of sorrow at the consigning
of the loved heart to the lonely grave,
was also the sighing sound of the central ice
unwilling, shifting deep, beginning to move.

Ours is the river on which the oxen were roasted,
where jubilant skaters undisturbed for years
performed their accomplished exclusive dances;
and fish wide-eyed were held chill hostage;
and none could count the numbers who perished from cold,
or stripped the fur from the living to keep themselves warm.

And across the ice ran disordered racking highways,
and over the ice rolled all of the nation's exchanges,
and falling on the ice were many whose limbs would not hold them,
whose skin showed in scars the dealings of the frost;
and drivers of high swift sledges furrowed the ice
as they made their determined journeys wherever they would.

And then, this sound: an ancient and ominous groan,
breath from the shivering glassy depths, a breaking
in harsh unbreakable places, the starting up
of a small, ineluctable flow. This sound: the moan
of the mourner, that guttered the candles and torches,
and loosed the wellsprings frozen at the source.

So now, across the standing ruins of winter,
grey sullage washing over ravaged landscapes,
we enter a world whose widening light reveals
the stunted, sturdy stretch of things still growing:
ice-age survivors, green, adaptable
to every bitter usage of the cold.

The air has softened, in-drawn breath hurts less,
and trees above the floodline are budding now;
birds with bright plumage have once more been sighted,
blades of grass are insistent underfoot,
and during the lengthening, strengthening hours of daylight
we meet, to encourage a likelihood of flowers.

*Stella Davis*
*Southampton Test CLP*

## Prisoner Of Conscience

He's a prisoner of conscience,
He wants to believe
That somebody cares,
That somebody grieves
For the lost and the lonely,
The weak and the poor,
But he can't see beyond
The prison cell door.

He's a prisoner of conscience,
They gave him no choice --
The promptings of conscience --
He had to give voice
To the things he believed in,
The truth he stood for,
So they locked him away
Behind a prison cell door.

We're all prisoners of conscience
In some small degree,
No matter how much
We may yearn to be free;
We're not living in freedom,
If we choose to ignore
The voice that is muffled
By the prison cell door.

*Andy Wood*
*Wirral South CLP*

## Lest We Forget

While you pontificate
About the state of readiness
For nuclear war,
Have you noticed that
There's little room
On the War Memorials
For many more names.

*John Risbrook*
*Southampton Test CLP*

## Images Of Industry

The factory gates are closed,
Caging a dinosaur's skeleton,
A framework of extinction.

Cranes stand rusting idle,
The dockyard's arthritic fingers,
Accuse the sea of absent cargoes.

The mine shaft cable hangs,
A severed tongue in chiselled throat,
Songs replaced by dusty silence.

*Michelle Reid (aged 17)*
*North Wiltshire CLP*
*In memory of her grandfather: Charles Reid*

## Green, Spleen – Unclean!

*(Sonnet on IRA . Written within a few moments at a London Bomb)*
Love came from above, at Christmas
Child, born of a love – not wed
A virgin, pure, fair – yet ringless!
Led to a Faith that thunders – "unwed bed
Causes damnation" Yet, to destroy
our northern view of "church" does claw
At every sick, sad, silly boy
With bombs and bullets – tools of war
Hate, for this different theme, is "good"?
For this was He, nailed to that tree?
(Strange sort of "good" raised from His wood)
Have you not thought:– sins of Love are small
Great sins of hate are devilry, and pall

*Sylvia Dixon Ward*
*Dulwich & West Norwood CLP*

## Join New Labour For A New Life, A New Britain.

Now span our lives so filled with strife
Forgotten poor, locked, bolted door
Our jobs held dear, blind hatred, fear
Sad surgery queues, depressing news
Families that part it breaks my heart
For things so bad the thoughts I had,
Britons why have we sunk so low
Both we and our tormentors know
But hark to this you who seek bliss
Say, say today there's another way
Away this strife, a better life
A life New Labour plans for us.
So shoulders high await good news
Why shouldn't we, a nation great
Become once more a foremost state
People contributing, stakeholders all
In work once more and standing tall
With our party great steering our fate
Let's show oppression the outward gate,
Look to the schools our children there
Let's treat them right, let's treat them fair
Succour the old and bring them joy
Reward the workers not just the old boy
Strive, strive for peace in our dear land
And once again extend the hand.
New Labour, yes you'll set us free
Your good for all your fine for me
So join together let's shout aloud
New Labour'll make our Britain proud.

*Cyril Saunders HCR*
*Chatham & Aylesford CLP*

## The Awakening?

I awoke in the middle of the night
    It was raining very hard
I could hear it very clearly
    As it fell in my back yard.

I thought to myself how different
    The sound of rain must be
To those who are so fortunate
    Who live in the country.

Who live in fine large houses
    With servants and much wealth
Who never want for anything
    Enjoying good education and good health.

I compared these with the multitude
    The working class as they are called
Who live to serve their masters
    But most of them are fooled.

Because it's not so obvious
    In these days of much money
Just who it is that's always stung
    And who gets all the honey.

The working class is always told
    That they alone are to blame
When things go wrong economically
    And its always been the same.

Years ago they'd hang you
    If you stole a sheep to eat
But they sent women and children down the mines
    So the rich could have their heat.

Years ago a little song
    Found itself great fame
"Its the rich that gets the pleasure
    And the poor what gets the blame".

And still it's just the same today
    Its the unions who are to blame
Who are responsible for inflation
    For this country's mess, so they claim.

It's the workers who cause the trouble
    When they lay down their tools
Not the profiteer or speculator
    Do they think we're fools.

To believe all their rubbish
    When they talk as though they were sages
When they tell us that prices
    Haven't risen as fast as wages.

They've now shown conclusively
    That profits are rising fast
So can you still believe them
    The greedy capitalist class.

But how to convince the people
    Is the greatest problem I thought
How does one bring about changes
    That's the solution I sought.

And so as I lay here
    In my bed in the middle of the night
It came to me, the answer lies with the workers
    To enjoy what is their right.

It's they who must fight for their benefits
    Of their labour and their brain,
But do you think its possible
    The capitalists might dissolve in the rain!

*Ron Spack*
*Christchurch CLP*

# Nostalgia

This winter time, with nostalgia
I think of the bygone days
When I was proud to be British
And proud of our British ways.

Now there is little I'm proud of
As I live through these long Tory days
Our people all scarred by unfairness
Of uncaring Conservative ways.

Services all diminished
Swamped by the market craze
Institutions changed into quangos
These are the new Tory ways

Parliament, once the mother
Sinking in sleazy haze
No one cares for the other
No pride in our British ways.

The only hope that I have now
To escape from this dismal maze
Is the clarion call of New Labour
To develop some new social ways.

To create again a Community
Of fairness, a trail we can blaze
To become once more just one country
Undivided, with New, British ways.

*Bill Stonebridge*
*Windsor CLP*

# The Iceman Cometh

Where heroes save on miser rate
And chill the aching bone
Where pension books are coldly bled
To those who live alone
I knew a man of eighty years
Who served his country well
He knew hypothermia
And with him England fell.

When winter ice embalms the old
The cost is seldom cheap
While self-made men sweat in bed
This land can never sleep
At Leipzig and at Arnhem
A soldier caught a cold
And now the war is over
His peace was glibly sold.

*Stephen John Singh-Toor*
*St Alban's CLP*

## Living In The 1990's

I found an old coat, propped up in the street
Inside an old man, stone cold not asleep
   I saw men in suits, walk by without care
   Ignoring the poor, wrapped in their despair.

Contractors were building a road over trees
Protesters ignored, their cries fall like leaves
   Nothing could stop the machines of destruction
   The roar of mechanical earthen eruption.

Looked to the dole queue, worn men out of work
A government uncaring, just misery and hurt
   The mines are run down, no work to be had
   The mania of money, the capitalist's glad.

The government sat, in gluttony and greed
Whilst violence and crime, power and sleaze
   Lay thick in the city, their power game lies
   Out in the ghetto, a starved baby cries.

I looked for the few, who call out for change;
A new party for people, yet alien strange
   The future is bleak, no matter the rules
   But never give in -- the Red Flag still calls.

*Byron Taylor*
*North Cornwall CLP*

## Bye-Election In The Sticks

The activists come from the big town today,
So we'll get them to canvass down Helden's Farm way.
    Let's hope that on one thing at least they are clear:
    You've got to use tact with us rustics...
        Oh dear,

This brother thinks everyone, everywhere, basks
In the sun that shines out of the T&G's arse;
    Here's a young Indian lawyer, with foot in the door,
    And he's now cross-examining old Mrs Moore;
There's a boiler-suit lady, acts very pale pink,
But if you're male gender she reckons you stink...

T&G's got psyched up for a shouting match
With an Uncle Tom worker who still adores Thatch;
    And as for our lawyer, his face has gone dark---
    Mrs Moore has just uttered a Racist Remark;
The man-hating lady was quite right, it seems,
For a very male dog's ripped her boiler-suit seams...

    Let's call all this off, have a jar in the Goat;
    We must limit the damage or lose every vote.

        *Robin Oakley-Hill*
        *Sevenoaks CLP*

## Interdependence

Under the dim green canopy of ancient trees
All Is connected, a chain of food, of birth
And death. Self sustaining, the forest lives and breathes,
Absorbs greenhouse gases. Its roots hold firm the earth.

All over the world, the trees are going,
As chainsaws shriek, forests cry out in pain.
Frail soil is eroding, the deserts are growing
And drought leads to famine after years without rain.

In beating sun, women walk miles to collect
Wood for their fires. Land is cleared for farms,
Timber is sold to pay interest on debt.
As they cut down their forests, we all suffer harm,

We are dependent upon our neighbours' trees,
A storehouse of wisdom, of infinite worth.
All is connected. we owe our debt. We must seize
Our chance to create a fair world, one earth.

*Wendy Ellis*
*Chichester CLP*


## The Hidden Agenda – Right Wing Dreams.

Now the cold wars over
Now the troops are home,
Now we are the masters
And will prove our hearts are stone.

Farewell to the NHS,
Goodbye to housing aid.
Now we are the masters.
And no longer are afraid.

Farewell the old age pension,
Goodbye to a steady job.
Now we are the masters
And know who we can rob.

Hooray; the rich will be richer.
Hard luck the rest will pay.
Now we are the masters
And know the game we play.

*Paddy Roberts*
*Saffron Walden CLP*


## People Still Die.

As a young man they sent me to war
And told me to fight for democracy,
Millions died, and they gave me a medal,
Oh god, what bloody hypocrisy!

*Mike Turner*
*Ruislip/Northwood CLP*

## The Dialectic: Pravda Vitezi

*"Truth shall prevail": inscribed on the wall of St Vitus's Cathedral Prague*

Tall stuccoed buildings and tramlines in the pavé;
In every decade history erupts, on motorbikes or in tanks.
People in tall apartments eat heavy meals, and wake
To see a new truth crush the pavé again.

Truth is a slogan stuck on the crumbling stucco.
Truth is freedom to bargain, truth is black, and truth is red.
Whatever lies on the tramlines with flies licking its face
Is a downright lie; the shovels are there to prove it.
Truth is that which shall prevail in the end.

Truth rises out of tomorrow like Venus out of the sea,
Shell-borne like her, exploding with naked grace.

When the last sunset leaves the last evening alone,
At the finish, who will remain to see
The final truth that has no mate to contradict—
The only virgin thesis, childless at time's end?

*Robin Oakley-Hill,*
*Sevenoaks CLP*

## Britons Never Shall Be

Henry Drake, still at school,
    sees his father put away
      for misbehaviour.

A teenager before the word is known,
    the army claims him for his country's fight
      for freedom.

Benghazi -- weather sunny, plenty grub.
    That's new, payment too.
      Peace intervenes. Home to Blighty.

Better off by one new suit he's free
    to find a job, low pay, and girlfriend,
      keen to save.

Romance falls through, but he gardens,
    wins prizes for dahlias, carrots, parsnips.
      Same job, same low wage.

When Henry Drake is forty-five --
   'Sorry ... cut-backs, but we ... thanks for
     Now he's free

to care for mother, ailing fast.
   She dies at eighty-one leaving him
     to stare awhile.

At least he's kept some hair.
   He'll look for ... join a ... make new
     but British men of Henry's station,

unprivileged, no decent education,
   find themselves ditched
     by a freedom loving Nation.

*Helen Heslop*
*Wansbeck CLP*

## The True Blue Privateers

The Jolly Roger flew high over the city
When they flogged off our assets without shame or pity.
As they lined their pockets with the peoples lolly
They honked, "the True Blues are generous and jolly".

There were perks for the wives, and jobs for the boys,
Champagne, cigars and executive toys.
Porsches, pretty ladies and expensive scent
And they built large offices no one would rent.

Fine country houses and villas in France,
Lots of money for games of chance.
Treble pay for directors of the boards.
And lots of free shares to add to their hoards.

Now the country's nearly broke
After squandering millions on the Poll Tax joke.
Billions more on the millions of jobless
Hapless victims of True Blue dogmas.

*P.Roberts*
*Saffron Walden CLP*

## Apologies To Lewis Carroll

"You are old, Tory Government," the young man said,
  "Experience should have taught you to be wise;
Yet you speak like idiots, not right in the head,
  With cat-calls and disorderly cries."

"These unconventional manners", they said with some pride,
  "Are meant to alarm the Opposition,
And the blunders, many and oft, to hide
  Of the Front Bench politician".

"You are old," said the youth, "as I mentioned before,
  And have determined on privatisation,
Although it is obvious, more and yet more,
  It will be of great cost to the nation."

"The use of statistics," they claimed with a stare,
  "Will show that our figures are right.
By making an adjustment just here and there,
  We are able to prove black is white."

"You are old," said the youth, "and can remember with joy
  The old Victorian days lang syne,
Forgetting, perhaps, that then many a boy
  Used to suffer in chimney and mine."

"Self-improvement," they made answer, concise and quick,
  "Is a Victorian idea, more or less;
We have no time for the aged or sick;
  They get in the way of success".

"We have dealt with these questions, and that is enough;
  We shall end this explanation.
We cannot listen all day to such stuff;
  We must get ready for our vacation."

*Mrs Joan Bligh*
*Chesham & Amersham CLP*

# Ode to the NHS

The N.H.S. is dying,
A slow and painful death,
When all it needs is money
That will bring with it new breath.

The nurses work long hours,
For a pittance of a pay.
Morale is at its lowest,
As they scrape from day to day.

We call our nurses "Angels",
On their dedication we rely,
Where would we be without them,
I'll tell you, lots of us would die.

They've been reduced to one day strikes,
Standing out on picket lines,
But the Tories show no mercy,
They've let them down so many times.

Why are the Tories insular?
So blind they cannot see
That by withholding money
They are killing you and me.

Soon we will all be going "private"
If the Tories get their way
But only pain and misery awaits
The ones who cannot pay.

We must keep alive the N.H.S.
Giving it the kiss of life
Injecting it with lots of cash
And ending all this strife.

I know that there will come a day,
Of this I will profess,
That hospitals will get their cash,
Long live the N.H.S.

*Linda Mumby*
*City of York CLP*

## A New Poem For New Britain

Please be careful–
this is a New Poem.
Separate, most distinct
from worn, loved
thumbed poetry
of the past.

This poem has
No Sharp Edges.
It conforms closely
with accepted standards
of rhyme, rhythm,
and style.

All Old Poetry
is Banned.
Please do not
associate new Poetry with
such outdated verse.
The consumer finds them

Unacceptable.
This Poem is malleable
and does not want to
cause Argument. That is
dysfunctional
to it's aims.

Please accept this Poem,
for it wishes
to be wanted
and is quite willing
to do so by
Cutting Old Throats.

*Byron Taylor*
*North Cornwall CLP*

## Stand And Fight

The pit wheel has stopped turning
So many lie silent now,
The shadow it casts over the village
Is one that destroys family life.

The miner looks in sorrow
At the pit, that was once his life
And wonders what he is to do
For his children and his wife.

The pit was where his father worked
And his father's father too,
He met his wife at the Miners Club
As her father was a miner too.

And now the village is dying
There's no money, nor work to do,
The shops are having to sell up and close
Which puts more people on the dole.

There is no other industry
The recession has hit that hard
So what can an out of work miner do?
Stand back and watch his village starve?

And now this Tory Government
Says more pits should be closed down
They seem set on destroying
This countries heart and soul

It isn't just the miners
This recession has hit us all
So now we must, as a country
Stand united to fight and heed New Labour call.

For if we stand and fight as one
This Government shall surely fall
And then we can build a country
Where there is work for all.

*Ms C J Hickman*
*Telford CLP*

## Energy Crisis In The Small Hours

A child walked into my dream
Pit-scarred and hungry; had there been bread in my dream
The child could have eaten. Alas, my well-fed body
Never fantasies food.

"My guts were smashed by a runaway trolley
As I pulled under the roof too low for a donkey's stoop.
Up in the air they had fed me with bits of Bible—
Cheaper than food".

I turned in my long warm sleep.
"Is it better out of the world than in?" I asked.
The child found this funny and spat on the floor of my dream.
"The coal masters thought that God

Would look after the likes of me, once under the sod.
(It was that let them sleep the way you are doing now.)
But it isn't so easy for them— I'm only here in your dream;
Time and the grave do not redeem".

The child dug deep in my mind and came up with bits of book-mash:
"There's something here explains it—
                              'external costs of an enterprise'
The coal masters thought the bill for the mess they made
Would be picked up by God and paid.

We wound up your spring, by digging your coal
—And now you've got oil and atoms—
But for every bit of work done, you spend a little more,
Till you wake and find yourself poor".

My dream began unravelling, like badly-wound string,
But I heard the voice receding: "The people yet to come
Will pay what's due to me and mine. God doesn't balance the book
That the coal masters cook".

I woke to find unravelling, like badly-wound string,
The oil-fired world making heat as it spun,
And I saw the sun labour, calling some of the children
To come and eat the food he's grown.

*Robin Oakley-Hill*
*Sevenoaks CLP*

## Mirrors And Bridges

I saw me on the street today
wearing another face –
though I was younger than I am,
a different sex and race –

at first I didn't know myself –
I had a different name,
though both of us were sensitive:
we laughed, cried and felt pain.

but soon I realised that I
and me should become friends
and work together patiently
'til wars and killing end.

The world is full of those who hate
the faces that we wear,
the tribes that we belong to, or
the way we wear our hair.

Some hate us in the name of God,
believing they are wise.
Our holy book is not like theirs,
and so to them it's lies.

But if there really is a God
outside the minds of men,
she can't be captured by mere words
that trickle from the pen.

And if, deep down, it turns out that
I'm you, and you are me,
then all this fear and prejudice
is quite illusory –

And if our hearts and minds can touch,
forgetting pride and shame,
we may learn that the things we seek
are very much the same –

I saw me on the street today,
a child of endless grace,
a part of life's infinity,
and recognised my face.

*Peter Hall*
*Mid-Bedfordshire CLP*

## The Lawmakers

They say they want peace, they don't want to fight.
 They make the decisions. They say that they care,
Which way is wrong and which way is right?

They build up their weapons, they build up their might
 To have equal numbers, to make it quite fair.
They say they want peace, they don't want to fight.

They talk and persuade so black seems like white.
 To safeguard our peace, for war they prepare.
Which way is wrong and which way is right?

Suspicions and fears can shut out the light,
 Oh, can't we build bridges and can't we all share?
They say they want peace, they don't want to fight.

Oh, can't we make friends? Can't people unite
 To use earth's resources? There's enough and to spare.
Which way is wrong and which way is right?

While millions are starving, refugees, in despair,
 They spend more on arms. Oh, how do they dare?
They say they want peace, they don't want to fight
 Which way is wrong and which way is right?

*Wendy Ellis*
*Chichester CLP*


## Deliverance

Church bells will ring in all the land,
'Red Flag' by Grimethorpe Colliery Band,
The countryside become serene,
More joy than there has ever been.

All the people of our nation
Will benefit from automation.
Market forces put to rout
When we get the Tories out.

Predators belong the jungle,
Let us then redress the bungle.
Everyone shall play their part
To give this land of ours a heart.

So come on lads and lasses all,
Answer to your leaders call,
Get your heads out of the sand
For deliverance is at hand.

*Arthur Wilkinson (Aged 81)*
*Wantage CLP*

## The True-Blue Herts Lad

One day while ditch digging with my Dad
He said to me be a clever lad
Always vote for the True Blue man
And you'll have a steak in your frying pan

I went to the polls with my mate Ron
And voted for Maggie and then for John
Who promised us steak in the frying pan
And said buy a house as soon as you can.

I took their advice and bought a fine house
Which I decided to call Happy Choice.
There was plenty of steak in the frying pan
And my wife often said "what a clever man"

And now I come to the bitter bit,
I lost my job and the house went with it.
My Wife ran away with a very rich man
And left me without a frying pan.

This is my story, this is my song,
Being True Blue was just a con,
And as for the thieving very rich man
He stole my wife, house and frying pan.

*Paddy Roberts*
*Saffron Walden CLP*

## Hopeful Political Requiem
## As Imagined By Michael Denzil Xavier Portillo

I enjoyed the Tory conference in nineteen ninety five,
    on the platform sat the very faithful few.
Some of them looked worried, some even looked alive.
    'till the one who stole the show came into view.

His rhetoric out-rhetoricked Willy Shakespeare,
    his choice of phrase, embarrassed S.A.S.
One expected Joan of Arc to reappear here
    to explain that she'd been burned alive for less.

And still Portillo went on unabated
    He flung taunts far and wide with great aplomb
all Europeans -- and most Jap's he slated
    (I imagined him in charge of neutron bomb).

Then I thought what could this lad do for new labour?
    in election year, he'd create party crisis
amongst Conservative's few friends and neighbours,
    IF: he wrote a manifesto of advice's.

## Just Imagine?

*He'd not be overpowered, not he*
*stealing parodies from Coward (E.G.):*

Don't put your family in N.H. Mrs. Bottomley
don't put your family in N.H.
You've reduced the waiting list
for exclusion of a cyst
by removing six at once with snooker cue,
then you saved us lots of lolly
leaving patients on a trolley
having heart transplants in store rooms. Didn't you?
So don't put your family in N.H. Mrs. Bottomley
Don't put your family in N.H.

I don't think John was mental
giving you Environmental
as the legacy you left behind lives on.

Matters not if the new lottery
goes to Branson or to "POT"ery
you are still attractive in whatever raiment.
If good treatment is the need now
Private medicine's the creed now
and as patients they must now take BUPA payment
So thanks Mrs Bottomley, but please Mrs. Bottomley
Don't put YOUR family in N.H.

## Political Requiem

*NOTE FROM DENZIL (inspired by Mr. Gilbert of G+S)*
*These thoughts to you Mike / I express.*

As most days it will happen that a victim must be found,
I've made a little list of those who won't be missed.
There's the poll-tax first offenders who will stay underground,
they never will be missed so I've scrubbed them off my list.
There's the pestilential homeless ones who go to ground like foxes
who never praise the government that lets them sleep in boxes,
all children who are late at school, should be at once foot clamped
and comprehensive schoolchildren should be in time boot camped.
Then bring back stocks, with thumbscrews,
and the whip none can resist.
To use them I insist
--- that's why they're on my list.

Yours hopefully: XAVIER Of Law And Order.

*Finally his advice to Mr. Major.*
*Wordsworth's worth a word.*

Stop wandering lonely as cloud,
your "SPELL" as P.M. is no more.
Behind you, waiting is a crowd
who's parentage you once foreswore
who'll swing the Tory AXE sometime,
then in leap I or --- Heseltine.
signed your LOYAL MINISTER.

*the late Jim Owen*
*Blackpool N and Fleetwood CLP*

## The Poverty And Plight Of The Cockleshell Heroes

What did the 'Cockleshell Heroes' do to offend?
The rich grew richer, the poor had nothing to spend!
Humiliating shame should bow their heads
Of those wallowing in riches on country seat beds ;
Medals for courage, medals for bravery!
Proudly worn, to cast into slavery!
Men risked their lives that others might live,
To be rewarded with medals – forcibly to give!
On a pension inadequate , utility fare,
Can one survive ? The chances are rare!
Forty pence rise, twelve months pending
Was lost through inflation of household spending.
The auctions at Sothebys plainly tell
Their precarious plight, which made them sell!
Professionals, executives, medics, M.P.'s
Add another nought to their salaries!
Is this what the war and sacrifice meant!
Pensioners with empty purses, down to the last cent?
Clothes from a jumble sale, outrageous high rent!

Television stands with dust covered knob
Inflated licence too high, (whilst some pay a bob).
Like a widespread epidemic, thrown in the pool
Telecom. Millions rose, who do they think they fool?
The largest donation set the world on fire,
Overpaid taxes which they didn't require!
Charities have flourished from the year dot,
The Queen Mother withdrew her donation, from the
                                    overflowing pot!
Can the local bodies pretend not to see
The plight of the pensioners – you and me?
Does it need a chisel or heavy hammer blow
To penetrate the skull that they might know?
Comrades of mine, as a Socialist born
Does the Red Flag fly spat on in scorn?
In righteous justice, ere the days go by
We must conquer and hold, look the world in the eye!

*Mary Dearnley*
*ColneValley CLP*

## Life's Hard

Little Boy and Little Girl–
Nice Mum– Nice Dad–
Nice Home– Nice School–
Playing in the sun.

Little Boy and Little Girl–
No Home– no School–
No Mum– No Dad–
Working in the sun.
No time to play just run.

Happy Women– Husband– Home–
Having hair done– holidays in Rome.
Sad Woman, just as pretty–
No clothes– no husband– no hope–
locked in a sweat shop
Like a beast of burden.

Happy Man, working– good job– nice wife
Golf on Sundays cutting big joints with a knife.
Sad man working all day long
For a few pennies, all joy gone.

Happy animals well fed and clean.
Sad animals alone and lean
Like the sad Girls and Boys
Rounded up one day and shot down like toys.

Will we come face to face
with who ever put us in our place
Next time perhaps to have
what this time we lack in life's race

*Pamela Meakin*
*Weston -super-Mare CLP*

## Human Race

What a chance the human race
When you see what we have done,
The man with the kind face
That kills for fun.

If people don't know who their brothers are
Animals haven't got a hope
and the plants end trees not a care.
If so called betters had no money, could they cope?
If things didn't make them rich would it make them care?

*Pamela Meakin*
*Weston-super-Mare CLP*

## Boiling Over

See the brown envelopes
pile up on a bare table.
A man is watching
the kettle boil over.
One in the afternoon
and still unwashed,
he looks at television
while dust collects.
A woman enters
tired and hungry
calling viciously
over unwashed dishes
and muck and mess
and no job and two jobs.
When she hit him
she thought of Thatcher
and couldn't stop.
A battered man
and a battered woman
lie clutching each other
no strength and wet faces,
blurred in the mist
of a steam-filled room.

*Billy MacPherson*
*Newcastle -upon-Tyne Central CLP*

## Jack

I sit soft in oil-fired rooms.
I'm all right, Jack –
How are you, Jack?

Seats at the opera,
Seats at the play,
Toss a coin to Jack
As I pass him on my way.

Can I sit serene
As I settle in my seat
While Jack sits out
On the cold concrete?

Home again, no Jack in my way,
I'm very annoyed by the train's delay.
I'm all right, Jack –
Where are you, Jack?
Jack's jacked it in on the railway track.

*Jean Cardy*
*Croydon South CLP*

## Truth

Wandering spirit of the wind
Release unto me the truth of men
Whose deeds have caused me to ask of you
You who have carried the words of "leaders"
Commanding others to tear at the heart of happiness
And so at the heart of the world itself
Do not mock me with your relentless whispering
That wears down both rock and man.
I demand to know what it is
That these first amongst equals require
To feed their self-interest fed fire.
Blow, blow to and fro not to fan these flames
But to extinguish them and scatter the ashes of truth
To the deceived of man and earth.

*Gerald Waters*
*Kensington & Chelsea CLP*

## My Classroom

My classroom's over-crowded there's an awful lot of din
I cannot get on with my work and the roof is caving in
So save me from the Tories my dearest Mr Blair
And save me from my teacher who is tearing out her hair.

*Keara Francis (Aged 10)*
*(submitted by mother, C A Francis)*
*Sherwood CLP*

## Cuba

*(After giving away soap,*
*toothpaste and Tampax in Havana)*
The children beg for soap
We are humble
From fine hotels
We watch your city crumble
But your people are not homeless
Your people are not hungry
We know that much and more
Remember the poor, before the revolution

A rich man's playground then
The rich play here again
On your terms
That much we see
From the safety, of a dollar economy

You have fought imperialism and a regime
We bring dental and feminine hygiene
On leaving, time only to embrace
In two weeks we have not become intimate
It's only cheek to cheek we kiss

But each morning as I brush away
The bad taste of my safe existence
And every time I bleed
I feel the passion in those lips.

*Sue Johns*
*Mitcham & Morden CLP*

## Green Shoots

You try for your wife,
For your children,
For yourself.
And you try yourself a life
From off the local library shelf.

At first the letters drop
Rejection gnaws,
Nuzzles in your guts
And grips inside.

But then the letters stop
For no apparent cause,
Life becomes a series of 'buts',
With very little option but to hide.

And you lie to your wife
To your children,
To yourself.
You pretend yourself a life
From off the local library shelf.

Your weeks turn into fortnights
Disappearing down a hole.
Lies become essential to your thinking.
As you walk with some pretence of pride
Down to the dole,
You fail to see the depths to which you're sinking.

And you cry for your wife,
For your children,
For yourself.
As you while away your life
From off the local library shelf.

*Andy Terry*
*Stoke-on-Trent North CLP*

## The Suffragette

A college reunion,
Some anniversary or other.
For prize guest they produced
An ancient, ancient suffragette,
Frail, tiny as a child.

With exquisite care,
They unwrapped the tissue-paper;
Solicitously, with silver tongs,
They settled her on her feet.
We prepared, with cigarettes and glasses,
To offer our ten minutes' tribute
Of reverential tedium.

An astonishing tenor
From that brittle
Birdcage of bones
Put out cigarettes,
Re-lit attention,

No canary this,
But an eagle.

"I'm not going", she said,
"To talk about suffragettes –
That's all a long time ago.
It's the Future I care about"

And proceeded, for an hour
To light for us torches
That glimmered further ahead
Down the dark tunnel
Than we had yet
Felt ourselves called
Even to peer.

I heard she died soon after.

I hope I go out like that.
*Jean Cardy*
*Croydon South CLP*

### The Hero's Return

We trace out most lives
    From childhood to grey hair.
At his height the Hero arrives
    And we read back to where

Boiled cabbage smell
Suffuses the stairwell.

Backwards we follow
    And tint his youth
With colours we borrow
    From a later, provisional, truth.

Lenin in a Zurich slum
    Makes notes and reads;
Careful people come
    To report, giving no leads

To the foreign police.
    There was, once, an apotheosis—
But only on short lease.
    It no longer throws light on this.

Anonymity preceded
    The tomb in Red Square.
That niche now superseded,
    He shuffles back to where

Boiled cabbage smell
Suffuses the stairwell.

*Robin Oakley-Hill,*
*Sevenoaks CLP*

## Challenge Of The Twenty-First

Born just before nineteen twenty,
I never could believe
That I'd outlive
The twentieth century.

It had so many years to go.
How could I ever know
When I would get the seal of doom
Perhaps while still in early bloom.

When I was due to be delivered
My mother clutched her sides and shivered
As she saw the Zeppelin glide
And feared stigmata would abide
Forever in my face.

Although this was the "wrong" end of the City
I came out pink and pretty
A veritable baby of the Peace.

But the stigmata really were in situ
Ready to surface when there was need to.
Three stripes and all unseen,
In my twentieth year
They emerged bright and clear
On a sergeant smart and keen.

The next page of the file
Tells of the sands of the Nile.
When Rommel ran
The rout began.

An interesting diversion –
Before our planned incursion
On to Italy's land
I wrote a poem long and grand
And won first prize
(for those days a substantial size)

Presented by Montgomery
With all the usual ceremony.
I quote "and the gentle eerie patter
Of sarcastic shrapnel asking what's the matter?"
Not bad I suppose – it rhymes!–
And a likely motto for our times.

But I jump ahead.
First came the dying and the dead,
The mutilated and displaced.
Our hopes rose high, our pulses raced.
If Jerusalem's a goal so dear
Could we not build Jerusalem here?

It must be said – we nearly did.
For schools, for health, we made our bid.
We did our best for those in need
But the mean in spirit disagreed.
The noble tide began to turn
Our long-held faiths we must unlearn
Our works began to come apart
Some, including me, were losing heart.

Last year I went into Emergency –
There was a blockage in my blood supply.
If I heed the warning and do things right
I can live to a hundred – I might, I might!

Here's the challenge I will now take on:
I vow to be present at millennium's end
To see this worst of all centuries pass on.
To its rat-bitten hole I'll send
This of all centuries most accursed –
And I'll turn my face to the Twenty-first!

*Tony Celner*
*Hendon CLP*

## The Forgotten Marchers

They tramped along the valleys, in those bitter days of yore,
Just like the iron men had done, a hundred years before;
With hearts so full of anguish
        and they'd lost most of their pride,
Thoughts of wives and children starving,
        some broke down and cried.

They came down from the hillsides, to join this ragged throng,
Out of terraced homes they tumbled,
        as the marchers went along;
With nothing in their pockets, their faces gaunt and drawn,
Told of hunger that they hadn't known,
        from the day that they were born.

They plodded on for miles and miles, the distance had no end,
Determined heads were held aloft,
        not a single man would bend;
They were marching on to London, to support the miners' call,
And they little knew that they had lost,
        before they reached Whitehall.

With heads hung low, they marched back home,
        with less than when they started,
They came back to the valleys grey, forlorn and heavy hearted;
No triumph this, the cause was lost,
        by those who should have fought,
To all of them who made the stand,
        their action stood for nought.

They were prepared to stick it out, to retain a decent living,
But when the deal was introduced,
        they weren't taking, they were giving;
'Twas back to work on harsher terms,
        that meant quite a cut in pay,
I wonder how many of you Union men,
        would swallow that today.

*Roy Harris*
*Islwyn CLP*

## For The Rights Of All

We've fought our cause for many years,
    From times when children worked like slaves,
When wives and mothers shed bitter tears
    Over loved ones brought to an early grave.

It mattered not, to the masters then,
    If men were killed, to increase their wealth,
Young boys and girls, eight, nine, or ten
    Worked long hard hours, which affected health.

Then life was cheap and conditions appalling,
    The working class then had just no say,
They worked from five to seven 'twas galling
    For just a mere pittance was their pay.

The Chartists took up the Labour fights
    To strive for all those who had no hope,
They shot them down, for demanding rights
    With which the masters could not cope.

The times have changed, but still we find
    Some masters who still rule by fear,
They cannot leave the past behind,
    They are autocratic and insincere.

We are carrying on in the Chartist way,
    Still mindful that men have their rights,
Opposed to discrimination in any way,
    When people have real freedom in their sights.

So rally round us, you Labour folk,
    And let all know we are not afraid,
We'll not be restrained by any yoke,
    Like our forefathers, who died, and paid.

*Roy Harris*
*Islwyn CLP*

# Fight On

The Chartists fought the Labour cause.
Against the owners rich and strong,
To eradicate the slavish laws,
That had them prisoner for so long.

Rise to the call you Labour folk.
Lend us your aid to win the fight,
To ensure we are never under yoke,
To the Tories, or any such like.

This Tory shower will wield and flail,
And have proved they will change the laws,
They'll even have us put in gaol,
To ensure they destroy the Labour cause.

But we will never like puppets be,
Tugged by whoever offers the best,
We'll say our piece, and be quite free,
To put resolutions to the test.

We'll never sit in the chamber there,
Afraid to speak for those we serve,
We'll have a go, and show we care,
And fight them with unflinching nerve.

The Labour cause is never lost
When comrades rally to our side,
Our forefathers fought, and to their cost,
Some laid down their lives, and died.

The struggle is still going on,
Where working class are slaves to greed,
They'll still be struggling when we've gone,
So join the fight and get them freed.

*Roy Harris*
*Islwyn CLP*

## Our Friends– "The Con Club"

They've been in power and the years have gone by,
  And just look at what they have done,
All prices have gone searing up to the sky,
  To the lower paid, it's not very much fun,

What good is a penny off the tax, to those
  who are now paying tax anyway,
Extra money on fuel VAT, they pay through the nose.
  For all they need day by day.

It's all right if you can earn forty thousand or more,
  You will certainly know who to thank,
For an extra two fifty a week, that's the score,
  You can laugh all the way to the bank.

With shares in the services, and BR too,
  They said profits were far too low,
So they pushed up the prices to me and you,
  And dealt us a real body blow.

It's never mind us, they'll look after their own,
  They make sure they are coining it in,
And when they have skimmed all the cream off the top,
  They'll let Labour clear the mess we are in.

They'll have made enough to last five years,
  'Til the country is back on the gain,
Them they'll put them back in, so have no fears,
  They will promise the same things again.

If your waiting for some sort of redemption,
  And for all our problems to be resolved,
You'll by waiting when you draw your pension,
  Because the Tories will not get involved.

To the workers, they're real CON artists,
  While they are in, you'll be kept under heel,
So we'll fight against them, like the Chartists,
  To let them know just how we feel.

*Roy Harris*
*Islwyn CLP*

## Red-Brick Landscape

Five people
surrounded
by red brick
and white washing
all still.

A woman stands,
arms folded,
staring into the distance
as another woman's talk
is going unheeded
so re-directed
to an open-faced child
who listens
but does not understand.
His face is smiling
and wide-eyed.
His mother's face is metal
and razor-sharp.

An old man is dancing
to an accordion
in the next street.
But it is a serious dance
of lost pride and industry.

The woman's talk is of
them and us
great truths in black and white.

The metal-faced woman
tightens her grip on the fence
and almost dreams
of freedom.
She'll get things done.
Keep on getting things done.
Keep on
accepting waste
and broken days.

She grips the smell
of beer and smoke
as she searches pockets
for money. Bills.

Her neighbour talks of
them and us
to forget her own nightmare.

The boy is still looking up
and smiling.

A girl further back
in crushed ribbon
and wellingtons
looks on and understands,
Later
she will remember
while her mother forgets.

Such a serious dance
on the wet cobbles
one street up.
What of her dance
when the music stops?

The girl in crushed ribbon
won't forget
white sheets and foul mouths
carpet beatings or black-eyes
hiding places or hidings.

The boy with the golden smile
will be trained to forget.
One day he will dance
his most serious dance
while others face the music.

*Billy MacPherson*
*Newcastle-upun-Tyne Central CLP*

## Ode To Thatcher

Mr Major's made it then,
That woman's gone at last;
It's time to view the legacy
Of these eleven years just past:

What did she leave to judge her by?
What wonders to unfold?
Is it true she stopped the rot
And turned our dross to gold?

The power of the miners gone!
They sorely tried her wits.
No union without miners; so
She simply closed the pits.

Boilermakers, shipwrights too,
Her plans they could have marred;
Thus in the north and west today
You'll scarce find one shipyard.

But ships are built and coal is dug
In countries far and wide,
Which haven't had the benefit
Of this lady for their guide.

Up in the north where ships once ruled
And men were proud and strong,
A Nippon car usurps their place;
Don't tell me it's not wrong

For men of skill and craftsmanship,
Developed over years,
To find themselves reduced to cogs;
There's matter here for tears.

Oh! I forgot, we kept the bomb,
Which in turn has kept the peace.
(Except in 'Nam, Korea, Goose Green,
And now the Middle East.)

"Of course the bomb has kept the peace!"
She shrilled, and shook her fist.
But tell that to the wives and loves
Of the men who now are missed.

'Sworn enemies' became best friends
To our pragmatic madam;
For when your friends are few at home
You look elsewhere to have 'em.

But look at home for homes not built,
At least not for the humble,
'Prestigious Dwellings' grace the 'courts',
And executives don't grumble.

If you have no roof at all,
And little prospects too,
Just pack your rags in plastic bags,
And a cardboard box will do.

For some there are who've made a pile,
And some there are with nought,
Who'll fill in forms for benefits
Which oft are soon forgot.

(If you got the reference
In the verse that you've just read,
Your school's no comprehensive,
You've 'opted out' instead!)

We're told our health's safe in her hands,
But beds and wards don't fill.
She claimed that they were treating more;
She must have made more ill.

'Law and order' was her claim,
She'd stick them all in prison,
How is it then that, after all,
The crime figures have risen?

"Inflation's high," the lady said,
"We'll bring it down for you!
The Labour Party is to blame,
Just watch what we can do."

Well, first she sent inflation up,
To a height not reached before,
Then she fought to bring it down,
But not quite to the floor.

As it came down the jobless rose
In numbers unforeseen.
But that's all right, there must be pain,
You all know what I mean.

Now up it goes, new heights are reached,
Let's see now, who's to blame?
Shareholders? No! Directors? No!
It's the workers' fault who claim

A wage enough to meet the cost
Of Poll Tax bills and such,
Of mortgages and rent demands
Which all become too much.

The Kurds could writhe 'neath poison gas,
And Israel crush the Strip,
But dare to touch our oil supplies,
We'll smite you thigh and hip!

If she is going to claim her 'reign'
Was the best we could have got,
It's only fair that she should then
Take credit for the lot.

*Fred Finney*
*City of York CLP*

## Lament To A Much Loved Labour Leader

*(on the death of JOHN SMITH)*

A man with whom I never spoke nor even met
Yet feel it as I would of any friend
That sadness of such tragic loss and deep regret
How such a truly decent man
Should meet with such untimely end.

*Anthony P Rowe*
*North West Cambridgeshire CLP*

## Preferential Differentials

It makes me sick to hear Tories say
That teachers and nurses don't need more pay.
What that achieves is more that leave,
More relatives left to grieve...

Patients are ferried from town to town.
There aren't enough beds – they've all closed down.
Doctors and nurses take the rap
The Tories have got them in a trap.

And when it gets right down to it
The admin guys will take their bit
Two and a half times what the nurses got;
Office hours and terms -- they get the lot!

There's not enough beds for intensive care.
The doctors are tearing out their hair.
British organs get sent to Spain.
British patients die in pain.

Teachers and nurses have got vocation
But the Tories use that for exploitation.
Divide and Rule their guiding text
Who knows what they're gonna do next?

There's nothing left to do but fight
If we want to set things to rights –
Fight and fight to get them out
And turn the next election to a rout!

*Frann Leach*
*East Ham CLP*

## In the Early Hours (April 10th 1992)

These days any excuse serves for a licence extension,
last night, at the White Horse;
it was the counting of votes for the general election.
They made a party of the thing,
hired a pianist
to encourage us to sing,
songs of real or imagined origin.
Ilkley Moor, The Lights of Aberdeen
I became a little restless
when they started on God Save the Queen.
But:
it was when some acned callow young Tory.
Opened his throat to bellow, land of Hope and Glory,
that in the words of the old time Sunday reporter,
upon proving the profession of some father's daughter
I made my excuses and left.

So here on the cold stone wall I sit.
Risking piles and pondering on the worth of it
and Newton's law of gravity,
as applied to both beer and whisky,
which requires each rise in price,
to be followed by a fall in quality,

until all that is left is the pain in the belly
which is not half as bad as the deep rooted agony.
Which lies in a baser part of my anatomy.
Alcohol and politics.
I swear that I will never touch either again.
Except perhaps, to ease the next five years of lower back pain.

*Criosdeagh Rhuadh*
*Southend West CLP*

## Thoughts On 'New Labour'

The name is really quite absurd
where are the labouring men?
There is no meaning in this word
we'll have to think again.

The 'Party of the Dispossessed'?
That shuts out quite a few
who, though they've feathered well their nest,
accept our point of view.

The 'People's Party' might express
our democratic aim,
but there are some it might distress:
the Soviets used that name.

What is New Labour? Who display
its most outstanding features?
The unemployed, the single mums,
ex-miners, typists, teachers,

Cartographers, computer buffs,
telephonists and doctors,
and booking clerks who've had enough,
dentists and dons and proctors

With such a varied membership
are we the Catholic party?
But who would fill a voting-slip
for Father Moriarty?

New Labour has a different face
to greet its second spring.
We'd better keep our name in place
we can't change *everything!*

*Joan Smith*
*Skipton & Ripon CLP*

## Political Rape of Wales

They made us go with them
Although we did not want to
Then they betrayed us with their words.
They took away our rights to run our lives
Then tied us up with silken cords,
Yet stronger than the ropes of previous years
They gagged our mouths and opened up our ears.

Each one in blue sympathised, but
Gave us nothing in return.
They said to the old "keep warm"
Yet gave no fuel to burn.
To the sick, an order to heal themselves
When doctors had no time.
They watched the mentally ill drowning
And did not throw a line.

"There are places for the poor" they said,
But all havens they destroyed.
They said "the wicked" would not harm us,
But with the laws they "toyed".
They took no measures to protect the weak,
They let the helpless die.
They called to memories of the old, the workhouse
And to the innocent they lied.

They wallowed in the depths of wealth
While many of those they ruled
Warmed themselves at a beggar's fire.
They gave no comfort to those who cried,
Whose misery was all they had,
Their homes had gone, their hopes had died.

They checked and sorted through the sick,
In case there might be some who were "quite well".
And though they saved money
to give handouts to those that had
They put the others through a living hell.

They raped the countryside
And gave us concrete roads where there had once
been solitude.
They destroyed simple homes of beauty
To build places far more crude.
They overturned decisions that the people themselves
had made.
They offered power where there was none.
They dared to call this democracy,
But it was rule by a minority,
And then they had the nerve to tell us we were free.

*Marian Flanders*
*Newport West CLP*

## Our Future

We used to sing a happy song
    When Labour ruled the land.
Sadly things have gone so wrong,
    Now Britons all must take a hand

Our hospitals are short of staff,
    Waiting lists are far too long,
Tired old doctors never laugh
    Whilst politicians beat the gong!

Can we carry on like this
    Short of bobbies on the beat?
Think of all the things we miss–
    In darkness lovers dare not meet.

I would solve so many things,
    Lottery millions I would take
Make us all like Queens and Kings
    Let every mortal share the cake.

With Tony Blair's assured command
    We'll walk towards a country new,
Marching on, a working band.
    Shares for all, not just a few.

*Beryl Shaw (aged 77 yrs)*
*Wythenshawe & Sale East CLP*

## Exploited

We work on a buildin' site, me an' me mate,
Time's knockin' on, we daren't be late,
Gaffer's waitin', watch in 'and,
So start up the mixer an' shovel in sand,
'Ave t' graft 'ard or we're on our way,
Sloggin' our guts out for a pittance o' pay;
'Ere comes the Boss, doff our caps,
Fill the water barrels, turn on the taps;
Joiners are workin', 'ear 'em saw,
Blisters developin', 'ands are raw,
Barrowin' concrete, my achin' back,
Can't show weakness, it'll get me the sack,
Got t' be as tough as teak,
Eighty 'ours worked this week;
Diggin' a trench t' lay a drain,
Wages are low, but daren't complain,
Money so pitiful it'd make y' sob,
Threatened that millions would love your job;
So into the mixer a bucket o' water,
Plus sand an' cement t' mix into mortar,
'od on your shoulder an' up a ladder,
Weaker, tired an' a little sadder,
Then down ag'in t' fetch more bricks,
Where men are navvyin' with shovels an' picks,
All day long the same routine,
Toilin' for employers so bloody mean,
Come the redundancies our names on the list,
We've done what was asked now we don't exist,
So off we go 'ome feelin' unwanted an' cheap,
Consigned, like so many, t' the Tory scrap 'eap.

*Steve Walmsley*
*Stockton South CLP*

## Relatively Unimportant:

For centuries the age old gap
Of right and wrong equations,
Was equalled by the handicap,
Of strained and strange relations.

The mothers of the brides in fact,
Are criticised indecently,
For purporting to hold a pact,
With Lucifer quite frequently.

Brides' dads it seems go quite unscathed,
Except to pay for workmanship
Of niceties bride's mum has craved
To satisfy one-upmanship.

The neighbour and antagonist
Is furious at mum's success
And even though in church they kiss,
The neighbour criticised mum's dress.

The feud continues unabated.
Neighbour flaunts her one son Jason
(Christ Church Oxford) educated,
Has a friend who is a mason.

As in this field mum can't compete
With literal confection'ry
So to the neighbour oft' repeats,
Tales of her hysterectomy.

Still families, neighbours, friend and foe,
Expose with rare intensity
How unimportant factors show,
How relative's our density.

Lastly after eighty years
Of studious negativity,
They bring forth "Einstein's" love affairs,
To dis-prove relativity.

*the late Jim Owen*
*Blackpool N and Fleetwood CLP*

# Banks Of The Tees

PART 1

Living on Teesside I used to see...
A landscape massed with heavy industry,
Where cupolas and chimneys, which towered so high,
Belched smoke and soot up into the sky;
For such was the sight along the River Tees,
Where ships which sailed the seven seas...
Plied their trade from far and wide,
Docking or sailing on every tide;
Arriving with cargoes which strained the keel,
They'd leave with holds full of iron and steel,
Made from ore mined in the Cleveland Hills,
Which supplied our steelworks and rolling mills,
Where, once it was forged, hammered and rolled,
Quality stamped, it was widely sold;
Exported to Europe, The Americas', Hong Kong,
Steel for Sydney Harbour Bridge – made by Dorman Long.

In foundries, moulders would make up their cores,
Sweating and slaving on sand strewn shop floors,
Whilst welders and platers down at Smith's Dock
Had so much to do they worked round the clock;
Midst a deafening staccato, dressers fettled and chipped,
Their finely honed chisels through metal plates ripped,
Alongside shipwrights, riveters, fitters and turners,
All gainfully employed, productive wage earners;
Proud men with skills, and though the work was so hard,
Felt secure in possession of a clocking-on card.

As cranes straining cables took up their lifts,
Hooters would signal the changing of shifts,
Then old cobbled streets, before they were tarred,
Bristled with humanity near every shipyard,
As hundreds of men, with their cans and bait bags,
Trudged into shops to buy papers and fags,
Hobnailed boots echoing and kicking up sparks,
Scraped at the pavements leaving permanent marks,

PART 2

Good old days? Halcyon Days? Many thought them so,
When evening clouds reflected molten metal's glow,
For industry bred community, hardship was something shared,
Comradeship eased life's burdens, someone always cared;
Gone forever now though, times when furnaces blazed away,
When hard graft guaranteed dignity with regular weekly pay,
When full time work was available and when almost every day,
A Tees built vessel eased gracefully into the river's spray.

Sadly, wilderness replaced this erstwhile, bustling scene,
Sites were levelled and abandoned where workshops had been,
Part-time, sweat shop employment was offered as consolation,
As malevolent Tory policy created a divided nation;
They tore out Teesside's heart and robbed us of our soul,
The devastation was appalling, as was the human toll.
A vibrant area was butchered and plunged into deep depression,
Callous Government excused itself by blaming world recession;
They told us that our industries were wastefully overmanned,
So a cut-back in employment was (intentionally) cruelly planned;
Then, in a cynical demonstration by insensitive, arrogant bosses,
Blatant intimidation was compounded with ruthless job losses;
No reason, no consultation, as our manufacturing base was lost,
Only padlocks, bolts and bars as a reminder of the cost.

An infamous slogan once proclaimed: "Labour isn't working!"
Accompanied by rabid accusations of 'layabouts' and 'shirking';
Later, a sanctimonious recitation of Saint Francis of Assisi's prayer
Promised EVERYONE... "Hope where once was despair."
But now millions of people stand idle and bored,
While the rich few use their wealth for investments abroad,
And this region, once famous for steelworks and coal,
Has an unemployed workforce on handouts and dole,
Whilst all that our craftsmen used to make here,
Is now made in Taiwan, Japan and Korea.

*Steve Walmsley*
*Stockton South CLP*

171

*The following two works were submitted by Christopher Hayes of Bolton NE LP and are extracts from a larger works*

## Boom Boom (You're Dead)*(taken from THE BOOK OF IDIOTS)*

out go the lights?
The Sewer King contemplates the complex issues of world minions,
seeks here and there from flatterers such agreeable opinions
as would turn a fisticuffs into a full blown Armageddon
and fulfil his shoddy, so-called saintly ambition
to rule the world: Faithless Lieutenant cringes by his side,
a grey man who rules a far off, insignificant isle,
who dreams of empires, and smiles a sickly saving grace;
envious rapture distorts his otherwise featureless face!
"A Special Relationship, sire, exists between yours and mine;
We two, together can Police this troublesome quagmire.
Your hand and mine in friendship, this whole world clasps,
Salvation, my Lord, from rank anarchy and collapse."
"Speak, lord Faithless Lieutenant, tell me what you see;
let the cause be just for such a dangerous prophecy,
(And make sure there's enough bankable readies in it for me!)".
The UnderTaker, of filth and world decay
exhumes the images of siege and ritualistic horseplay;
here and there maniacs seize the initiative of another uprising
to murder millions and impose another ruthless cleansing!
A story! A story! The Sewer King dictates,
and shoves his Fool back out, onto the stage
to earn his keep in one more extrapolation of altered states;
"My Lord, you do me more than my slight skill deserves!
yet the more of dreams unfold a sorrier state of affairs.
Who could resist the solid foundation of this integrity?
A whole Nation believes it is the benchmark of
                              international morality,
righteousness and honesty: a second coming, a twentieth century
new messiah in a land of golden opportunity.
Sits in Judge and Jury, dispenses judgement circumspect,
fawns to its allies and potential overseas markets,
(hoards to itself it's most Profound Military Secrets!)
be-metalled, as a modern knight of the quickening death,
bayoneted end forward,
searching for that Herald of your last breath on earth,
head filled to bursting with Confidence's confident sayings,
you heave about and deliver honourable, indecent slayings".

*Christopher Hayes, Bolton NE CLP*

**In The Slip***(taken from) NOW, VOYAGER !.)*

*.....an odd collection of loose affiliations.....*

Beneath the hurly burly of affluent everyday living,
in dark catacombs, draughty halls and tunnelled light-dancing,
gloomy sculleries pitted in the hasty birthings,
where the dark solidifies and gives birth to a brand new changeling.
A might of would be arms, that could arise a while
and explode this shallow complacency of lies.
Here's a paradox: living in the sense of how rotten things have been
a whole crumbling nation has passed by amongst us, unseen.
In cramped cardboard lodgings scattered on the ground
fake Prophets discourse and false Confessions abound.
Enshrined in holy script, this modern testimony,
a writ of fulsome providence, a beggar's elegy.
Dream weaver, sleeper, lies content inside the dragon's maw, and
though rhetoric damns, he could really tell you what he saw!
A dozen claims upon his weakened susceptibilities
from "Charities" queuing one upon the other to lighten his
terrible duties.
But in his paper rest, the cold and damp's retreat,
the dirt clings like spittles of disgust at every crease,
and every day dawns bright and empty, full of vacuous content;
too ill to dodge the ignorant and the opulent
he shambles each day through the subterfuge, beneath the
respectability
that seems to stare at him through the glass walls of another City.
Does your pity reel at such progress ill bred?
such claims are really just a guide to light their weary way to bed.
Captains Courageous ! Industry's salacious seamen,
sextant in hand, the whole world to command,
reefed in lagoons of scandals and collapse
so a few more pennies can fill their filthy grasp.
In due season summoned to the Royal Rout,
the Crown Imperial and bursting bank account.
The thrill of it all, face to face,
the blunted axe of fraud's latest candidate.
Amongst the hierarchy petty larceny's back in vogue,
a solitary vermin to precede a common plague;

*Christopher Hayes,*
*Bolton N E CLP*

## Democratic Interpretations ?

Juggling with semantics,
by Ian Lang, in ninety six,
was used by him to then extort
exposures from the Scott report.

Although the truth was oft' abused
he blatantly and strongly used,
an excess of superlatives
even for Conservatives.

He told Rob' Cook, "To understand,
that Waldegrave's job he can't demand"
and Mr. Cook is quite uncouth,
to say Will's lies were not the truth.

He advised victims not to gripe,
about Iraq's illicit pipe
as it wasn't Lyell's intention
to really put them in detention.

As forcing colleagues all to sign
and to toe the party line,
his use of national security
would surely give them all immunity.

For those of you confused by now,
who'd like to come to terms somehow
and bring a precedent to hand,
TRY "Alice in Westminsterland"

Cast "John" as Alice if you will,
(He admirably fits the bill)
wandering in complete confusion,
to cultivate "Feel-good" illusion.

That Waldegrave and Lyell might be,
Say TweedleDum and TweedleDee
and could as such act comically
to preach truths, economically.

When faced with conscience paradox
"MAD HATTER" of the golden locks
declared "As president, I'll not
sign secrets pledges with this lot".

This threw the party into panic,
criticism turned them manic
by losing in this complex game
who was there left for them to blame?

So Cabinet strives to amend,
as fearfully they comprehend,
the truth condemned as metaphysics
suggests Scott wrote in hieroglyphics.

*the late Jim Owen*
*Blackpool N and Fleetwood CLP*

## Klaptin

'This planet's nearly finished now –
for life it isn't suited'
the experts said to Klaptin, 'Sir,
the food and air's polluted
and the boys in the labs have just found out
they can't be substituted'.

Klaptin climbed in a rocketship
with a few of his richest friends,
told the press he was bound for Mars
to study economic trends.
'I'll be back for the world some day
but call me first if it ends.'

Klaptin went to the devil first
'Mister, I want to sell
this lump of garbage'. The devil asked
'Will this stuff burn well?'
'We've burnt it up already.'
'Then it ain't no use in hell.'

Then he bargained with the Lord
in the firm The Firmament & Co.
He said 'Our planet's finished now.
I guess it served us plenty.
So Mr God, how much in cash
can you give us back on the empty?'

God tossed the world in his hand a bit
just like an old potater
'No use to me. Just look at that'
replied the great creator:
the huge words 'NON RETURNABLE'
stamped on the equator.

*Gabriel Chanan*
*Windsor CLP*

175

## Pushed So Far

No I don't mind if you smoke.
Well I do actually.
But seeing as it's you –

No I don't mind if you're racist.
Well I do actually.
But I don't want to make a fuss.
It's hard to be unpleasant when you're face to face.
But I do object when other people do it,
people I don't know.

No I don't mind if you pollute the whole place
with your stinking deregulated chemical fertiliser factory.
Well I do actually.
In fact I feel very strongly about it.
But seeing as how I'm benefiting from it myself
at least that's what they say, though I can't see how
I wouldn't want you to think I'm taking the moral high ground.
But I think it's only fair to warn you
I'm going to send a donation to Friends of the Earth.

No I don't mind if you make billions out of Third World debt.
Well I do actually.
But it's embarrassing to get on my high horse about it.
After all, we've all got our little foibles.
I wouldn't want you thinking I'm politically correct.

No I don't mind you voting for another tax cut
even if it means starvation benefits, more homeless on the
streets and higher crime.
After all, it's a democratic country.
You're entitled to be stupid, selfish and short-sighted.
I wouldn't want to try and make you feel bad about it
and actually the extra cash would come in handy for me too
so long as I've still got a job
in fact I was only saying the other day
I'd like to be able to buy more books
on the crisis of the world economy.

Oi!
What do you think you're doing?
I saw that parking place first.
I know my rights.
You've bloody well stepped over the mark this time.

Right.
That's better.
Well just don't do it again.
Sorry I yelled but you know how it is.
A man can be pushed just so far.
No, it's all right now.
We can still be friends.
No, thanks, I don't smoke, but you go ahead.
I don't mind.
Well I do actually.

*Gabriel Chanan*
*Windsor CLP*

## Eighty Years Young

Today I became an octogenarian,
I was awarded a magnificent rise,
The princely sum of twenty five pence
'Twas more of a shock than surprise.

What shall I do with this generous amount?
Do I spend it all in one go?
Or eke it out with caution and care
To leave me an ample cash flow.

The options there are so many
And problems, they will arise,
To tackle this serious question
It will surely need expert advice.

I'm not interested in being affluent
With millions and millions stacked high,
But I would like just a little bit more,
Before the day that I die.

*Martha Prescott*
*Scunthorpe CLP*

## Leg End

It was a historical accident
that in the Republic of Transruritania
the National Matchbox Collecting Council
became so powerful, while other lobbies
like housing, welfare, health, employment
were regarded as the hare-brained obsessions
of outlandish minorities.

No doubt it reflected the key importance
of matches in the country's culture.
With no electricity, candles were all.
Every village had its matchbox industry
like wines in France or cheeses in Switzerland
and the wife of the national hero
who led the country to independence
in the turmoil of 1919
was so committed to matchbox collecting
because of a poignant childhood memory
that she slept with all the cabinet ministers
(including what few women
had attained these influential posts)
till they agreed to the vesting of supreme powers
in the Grand Convocation of the NMCC.

Now if you have an important initiative
that needs funding in Transruritania
you have to frame it in matchbox terms
or be driven to the fringes of opposition.
There's the National Institute for Social Welfare
Through Matchbox Collecting, The Royal Academy
for the Arts and Sciences of Matchbox Collecting,
the Department of Housing for Matchbox Collectors,
and as we speak the Grand Military Command
for the Defence of Matchbox Collecting Peoples
is mobilising for a crisis in relations
with the Kingdom of Petrolcouponia
who from time immemorial have persecuted
their matchbox-collecting minorities.

There's a Transruritanian legend
that beyond the Phantasmagorian mountains
lies an even more hostile civilisation

whose culture is based on human rights.
Should this ever prove true they vow to unite
with their Petrolcouponian adversaries
till the common enemy is vanquished.

For as their ancient proverb says,
'Share thy sword with thy neighbour till the monster be slain
then when thy neighbour observeth not, grab it back again.'

*Gabriel Chanan*
*Windsor CLP*

## Ants

I feel guilty
>    When I attack ants with kettles of boiling water
>    And puffer packs of poison,
>    Sending them in frantic hurrying desperation
>    To get out of the pain
>    Or back to succour the nest.
I won't pretend to more guilt than I actually feel.
>    Still, I don't like to lift a stone
>    And see the cracked tunnels,
>    The rows of dead eggs
>    And what looks like anguish
>    In the survivors.

Slick similes and slack, macrocosmic reflections
Come flocking,
But I don't care all that much about ants,
Nor do I really believe some extra-terrestrial being
Regards me as I do the ant.
Only this hits me:
>    When our masters destroy my college
>        Or your factory,
>            My job or your newspaper,
>                My village or your ancient way of life,
Does it cost them, I wonder,
>        Even as many pangs and misgivings,
>            As much unease of conscience
>                As my ant-killing costs me?

*Jean Cardy*
*Croydon South CLP*

## Turning Mother, 1989

Cycling through town at midnight
to turn my mother round:
cobalt clouds on grand manoeuvres,
an epic silently unwound
by my squeaky wheel on the gravel path
between the social services hut
and the sign on the multinational's fence:
*We regret no children beyond this point.*

To turn her onto her better side
to feed her pills with a scrap of fruit
from the mottled silver eggshell-thin
teaspoon, last of her trousseau.

Not so much a role-reversal
more a film wound backwards:
each of the baby's gestures wakes
another ribbon of the landscape.
Mother's weakening fingers sign
closing-in horizons:
the chair that can no longer be shifted
the casserole dish that can't be lifted
instruments turned to obelisks.

Half past midnight. Cycling back
the streets are avenues of thought
unknown to the throttled day.
*We regret no children beyond this point.*
Shivering now. If I'd come by car
I would have had news instead of clouds:
government welcoming people power
in Eastern Europe and bluffing here
they've just invented community care,
teaching their grannies to suck eggs
but still not giving them heat for life.

Eternal streets, not truly known
to me till now. As new as glasnost
and as old. The biggest change
in any life what it always was:
realising with astonishment
things that have always been there for others.

*Gabriel Chanan, Windsor CLP*

# It's Now Up To You

The caller up bangs on the slate,
On the wall, by the side of the door,
The answer as always, "Aye, I hear you,"
At dawn, the day starts as before,
It's pit hoggers, muffler, and tin water bottle,
Already to go down the hole,
It's crawl on your belly in a water filled seam,
To hew out the black demon coal.

The Minister bangs on the pulpit,
Preaching hellfire damnation and shame,
The answer as always, "Aye I hear you,"
But it's hard when there's nothing to gain.
It's Friday, it's Rechabite night
The sixpence for dues leaves little for food,
Methodism or Marxism,
The choice must be made, the decision be shrewd.

The mine owner bangs on the table,
He will pay no more for a shift,
The answer this time, "Aye you will,"
Never slaves again down your drift,
It's Banners and bands at the gala,
With Hymns soaring up to the heights,
Give thanks to our God and the Union,
For now we have Freedom and Rights.

The politician bangs on the podium,
He is there to continue the fight,
The answer as always, "Aye, I hear you,"
Keep hold lad, stand firm for what's right,
It's because we stood up to be counted,
You have been given the right to speak.
So it's now up to you the young and the new,
To give help to the strong,
for God will give help to the meek.

*Jean Moir*
*City of Durham CLP*

# Culture

The newsagent puts out his petals
brightly in the morning,
every leaf a glossy girl
they cascade about the awning.
There the seekers forage
hard upon their porridge.

Beside the ample bosoms
are massacre and famine.
Between the legs in garters
are tyrant men pretending
that they alone are saviours
especially of women.

A warrior carries off his prize
into the National Gallery
thirty thought-provoking thighs
that sap resolve and salary
rolled up in The Times
with other unsolved crimes.

Venus and Mars are juxtaposed
in this renaissance painting.
Her thighs are bare, her eyes are closed
but he is hesitating.
The explanation is he knows
one loses strength in mating.

A servant holds his armour
all ready to be buckled.
His shining sword lies ready
to aid him in the struggle.
Behind him dust is billowing
from the field of battle.

The bower where she stretches
is welcoming and floral.
Her flesh is soft and nourishing
to undermine his quarrel.
But he must resist her
to win his bloody laurel.

The catalogue says the picture
is a timeless metaphor
for noble masculinity
but how can one ignore
as some would argue bitterly
it glamourises war?
Can there ever be an Italy
however painted prettily
above moral law?
The artist is a felon.
High and low and old and new
the images of street and salon
choke us with the selfsame brew.

*Gabriel Chanan*
*Windsor CLP*

## Iron Lady Meltdown

Only when she fell
did I light Margaret Thatcher.
Golden locks
dripped wax
heavy
from the fire
in her head
onto Tory cheekbones.
Each drip a tear.
Each tear a celebration.

Shiny-wet
Spitting
Image
features
collapsed
drip dry.
Onto pin-stripe and pearls.

I smile as I imagine
her waxy mouth say
"The lady's not for burning. U burn if U want to".

*Billy MacPherson*
*Newcastle-upon-Tyne Central CLP*

# Awa' Cons Awa'

*(after Robert Burns – Awa' Whigs Awa')*

*(Chorus.—)*

Awa' Cons awa'!
Awa' Cons awa'!
Ye're but a pack o' greedy louts,
Ye've done nae gude at a'.

Our schools they flourished fresh and fair
And bonnie bloomed our nation;
But Cons came in like frost in June,
and spoiled our aspiration.
Awa' Cons &c...

Our ancient crown's fa'en in the dust—
They've blinded us wi' money!
A penny off will make us rich
But they'll be in the honey.
Awa' Cons &c...

Our sad decay in church and state
Surpasses my describing:
The Cons came o'er us for a curse,
An' we hae done wi' thriving.
Awa' Cons &c...

The NHS was doing well
And treatin' all our ailments
The Tories said they'd make it pay
And switched it to derailment.
Awa' Cons &c...

The coal seams were our nations blood;
The miners kept it pumping.
But Tory vengeance overcame:
We're doled, and Poles are dumping.
Awa' Cons &c...

Grim vengeance lang has ta'en a nap,
But we may see him waken:
God help the day when Tory heads
Are down and overtaken.

*(Final Chorus)*
>Awa Cons awa'
>Awa Cons awa'
>Ye've led us all a merry dance
>We're glad to see ye fa'.

*Derek Alan Taylor*
*Stafford CLP*

## A Dirty Tale

>Tory voters have been heard to say
>>The dirt is still a-flying
>And some MP's so bright today
>>Tomorrow may be sighing

>For in the House of Commons
>>The Tories no longer are sure
>That they can pocket a thousand quid
>>And not be shown the door

>Politics now is no longer fun
>>With whips breathing over your shoulder
>Some even suggest there's work to be done
>>And the opposition get bolder and bolder

>And people out in the sticks
>>Are really not playing the game
>They object to us picking up chicks
>>And say we have no sense of shame

>Some Tories are making it plain
>>They intend to cut and run
>All they ask is a seat on a quango
>>And a villa in the sun

>Or maybe a place in a merchant bank
>>As an executive director
>Anywhere, to be quite frank
>>Well away from the bloody elector.

*Bill Westall*
*Shrewsbury & Atcham CLP*

# Who Am I?

Who am I? I'm the one who there's plenty of room for In the hostels,
but, what about a place of my own? I have my pride you know,
But this Is government policy, I'm the scum of the land,
back to the streets I go,
I've no shares in British Gas, or the Power Industries,
or the Water Companies, or any of the rest,
I'm one of the ones left out, ignored, second-best.

Who am I? I'm the one who sleeps on the floor in the corridor
because there's no bed available at present.

My operations due today, but it's been put off because the
money's gone, at least I think that's what they meant,
Something about a rationalisation programme,
the ward has to close till March next year,
What happens now then, go home till then,
will they even notice me here?

Who am I? I'm the schooled, about to leave for a future that's
nothing but bleak?
Training programmes, work experience, "a chance to learn",
a chance to be paid bugger-all per week!
Of course I'll work hard,
of course I'll be listening and do what you suggest,
But hey, wait just a minute,
I'm a human being as well you know, I can only do my best.

Who am I? I am a simple human being who will help other
folk, no matter how much in the bank, how many
Directorships, how many Company shares,
But there's the Majorite "classless" Society, with two tiered
structures of Education and Healthcare,
If you've the money, and the pedigree and the background,
you're in,
They like each other you see, support each other's policies,
defeat the outsiders before they even begin.

Who am I? I'm the animal that God created,
in His Image, to do what he wished for the World,
I'm not Tory fodder, to be used
by the well-fed bosses with their hidden agenda's unfurled,
We need a government that cares, for all,
not just for a chosen few,

Ask yourself the same question, has the country gone wrong
in the past decade and a half, you'll know the answer, I do.

Who am I? I'm the one who will win the day,
Face it soon Mr. Major, your Government's had its day,
The dark days are nearly over, only a few more months to wait,
And If not before Mr. Major, in mid 1997, you and your lot
meet your just fate.

Who am I?  I am Civilisation. Welcome back.

*Philip Kendall*
*Crewe & Nantwich CLP*

## Tory Glory

The Tories, last election day
Said "Vote for us, vote all the way,
   We'll cut your taxes, wait and see,
   And lead you to prosperity"

Most believed them, you'll agree
So gave them a majority
   Too soon the truth we had to face
   We fast became the forgotten race.

The promises they made are dead,
Two million unemployed instead.
   More taxes, and it's very clear
   The crime rate's rising every year.

They're waiting for the FEELGOOD factor,
Scared to death of the Social Chapter
   It's very plain their master plan's
   To subjugate the working man.

We'll leave the Tories in no doubt
We put them in, we can boot them out.
   If they win again there's nothing surer:
   The rich get rich and the poor get poorer.

It's hope we need not more despair
New Labour-- led by Tony Blair.

*Dorothy Hall*
*Bristol North West CLP*

## Values

Children are starving in Somalia.
You worry that your hair is turning white
And colour it.
Whiten the earth with bones,
Colour the soil with blood
In sad Somalia.

Children are dying in the Balkan lands.
You worry that you cannot mow your lawn
Because it rains.
Red is the rain of fire
Where people are mown down
In the bleak Balkan lands.

Children are orphaned within Africa.
You worry that your weight is moving up
And check the scales.
"Slim" has a hollow ring
Set in the scale of death
In AIDS – scourged Africa.

Children are murdered in Brazil's vast land.
You worry at your package supplement
When sterling falls.
Look at that packaged child –
Dead on a garbage dump
For Brazil's tourism.

Children are prostitutes in Thailand's towns,
You worry that your train is late
And bite your nails.
Too late to save that child –
Nails painted, scented skin –
From Thailand's whorehouses.

Children are molested on Britain's shores.
You worry that your cat marks muddy paws
On your clean floor.
Pause to reflect that mire
Inflicted on young minds
Will never be wiped clean.

Children are sorrowing across the globe.
I see them on my television screen
From my cocoon.
I empathise their tears
And speak of their despairs --
But stay outside their world.

*Beryl Cross*
*Brentford & Isleworth CLP*

## The Magic Vote

How I love my country
She is mine by right of birth,
When looking at life elsewhere,
I appreciate her worth.
However, now there is so much wrong,
through out these lovely lands,
Are health and education,
Safe in Tory hands?

Whilst the unemployed and homeless,
Can see no great success,
But in spite of all the rhetoric!
We still seem in a mess.
When Labour is in power
So much will be fair and right,
But we cannot expect a magic wand,
To change all over night.

We cannot expect a magic wand,
But a commitment to what is right,
For people to have social justice,
Labour will always fight.
Whilst those who help the victims of crime,
Should not be punished I beg,
Whether public or policemen,
Or soldiers Like Private Clegg.
The answer to put things right,
To put things right I quote,
The nearest thing to Your magic wand,
Is for Labour, Cast your vote.

*Arthur Tree*
*Reigate CLP*

## The Major Who Has No Votes

*A "Redwood" Leer creation*

The Major who has no votes
Had once as many as we;
When they said, 'Some day you may lose them all,'
He replied, 'Fish fiddle de-dee!'

And his Auntie Heseltine made him wear
Rose pink spectacles, made with care.
For she said, 'The world in general notes
There's nothing so good for a Major's votes!'

The Major who has no votes
Flew across the English Channel;
But before he set out he wrapped his notes
In a piece of old grey flannel.

For his Auntie Heseltine said, No harm
Can come to his votes if his notes are warm;
And it's perfectly known that a Major's votes
Are safe – provided he minds his quotes.

The Major flew both fast and well,
And when birds or planes came near him
He tinkledy-binkledy-winkled a bell,
So that all the world could hear him.

And all the Members of Europe cried,
When they saw him nearing the further side,
'He has gone to fish, for his Tory friends
To secure their party political ends!'

But before he touched the shore,
The shore of the English Channel,
An ancient albatross carried away
His wrapper of old grey flannel.

And when he came to observe his seat,
Formerly garnished with votes so neat,
His face at once became forlorn
On perceiving that all his votes were gorn!

And nobody ever knew
From that dark day to the present,
Whoso had taken the Major's votes,
In a manner so far from pleasant.

Whether the sleaze or prisons grey,
Or crafty Labour stole them away –
Nobody knows; (and no-one emotes)
Over what became of the Major's votes!

The Major who has no votes
Was placed in a nice wheelchair
And they drove him back, and ferried him off
To his Auntie Heseltine's lair.

And she made him a feast at his earnest wish
Of peas and cyanide fried with fish;
And she said, 'It's a fact the whole world notes,
That Majors are happier without their votes.'

*Frann Leach*
*East Ham CLP*

## A Psalm to Pcelebrate the Psecretary of Pstate for Education

Gillian Shephard is my Lord therefore shall I lack everything.
She shall feed me on Tory propaganda
And lead me forth beside the waters of discomfort.
She shall try to convert my soul and bring me forth
In the path of Conservatism for her party's sake.
Yea, though she stalks the corridors of power,
I shall fear no evil: for the NUT is with me,
Its root and its branch comfort me.
She shall prepare a syllabus for me
Which shall trouble me: she shall fill my head
With reforms, yet my pockets shall be empty.
But her right-wing policies shall dog me
All the days of my life,
And she will, no doubt, dwell in the House of Lords
Forever and ever.
　　　Amen

*Kenneth Kaylor*
*Blaby CLP*

## Put it Down to the Tories

They sold Council houses, some people said thanks.
But now who's the owner? You've guessed it, the banks.
Can't pay the mortgage, can't pay the rent.
There's nothing left but to live in a tent.
They cut the tax mortgage relief.
For me, this was beyond belief.
They cut income support for mortgage interest.
And everyone will remember the rest.
The pits have closed, we don't want the coal.
And as a result we sign on the dole.
Education far all, go to top of the class.
But, it wasn't for me, 'cos I'm working class.
Political parties, I've heard, all alike.
All you have to do is, get on your bike.
The Tories can't be trusted to run the NHS.
But lots of Tory nurses helped to put them there I guess.
We were way out ahead on the opinion poll,
And then we were left to pay the toll.
I'm not relying on winning the tote.
But take it from me, I'll always vote.

*E Cowrie*
*Sherwood CLP*

## King Pound

*(Major and Clarke kneeling at the feet of enthroned King Pound)*
Who crowned The POUND, for all to revere?
To detain at it's pleasure all conscience and fear.
Supreme Judge and Ruler – decider of fate,
Democracy wither – Humanity wait!

Marvel at confidence certain as this,
Unlived potential, talent dismiss.
We don't all need fulfillment, pride and a choice,
Too complex a vision – Too many a voice!

We thought it best to let POUND decide
Who prospered from riches, who struggled and died.

*Paula Gwyer*
*Beckenham CLP*

## State Of The Nation

I can't believe the state our country's in
What shall I start with, where do I begin
We'll start with the aged we're supposed to care for –
They are left alone if they don't answer the door.
Do they care if they've fallen on the floor?
"No one answered so I went away,
But we did call every day".
Put them in a home, give them some dope
You number their days – is there any hope?
If you've saved enough they'll look after you well
But if you're poor, only time will tell.

Those are the policies the government have made
Survive if your rich – to hell with the low paid
Its not a risk working long hours
This shows the difference between two separate powers.
One's for the workers the other for the high class
Why should we struggle to keep them in top brass?

You come to an age where you don't matter anymore –
"Thanks a lot, now there's the door"
Is this all I can expect when I'm old –
You politely kick me out of the fold.

Then there's the people who've done nothing wrong
Put behind bars, left for so long.
Then someone comes bearing a key,
All of a sudden they find themselves free.
"Off you go now, there's a good lad".
You don't care that what they feel is bad.
Never said sorry for all their trouble.
They needed our help once, now they need double.
Coming to terms with now being free.
Are we all so blind, or don't you want to see.
End of the line – it's all so abrupt.
All the Government is lies and corrupt.

Then there's the hospitals, where people die
'Cos there's not enough staff. Can you tell me why?
You're trying to push us into paying private.
(Long John Silver was also a pirate).
Hospital beds and equipment not manned,
Is all this what the Conservatives planned?
*Margaret Newton, Rother Valley CLP*

# Windows

Windows
In need of cleaning
half concealing tower blocks
distant parkland

The old ways are best
Newspaper dampened
        Paper and ink

Tabloid centrefold
Inches from flowing water
His face
War victim
Famine victim
Drought victim
        Skin and bone

Eyes pleading
In my well stocked kitchen
Inches from flowing water

It's just a picture
        Paper and ink
        Skin and bone

It's just a picture
I fold it over
Under the water

On the other side
Trivia
Royal gossip
Princess Di
She goes to the window
No more dirt in his face
        Paper and ink

Outside nothing's changed
Barking dogs
Chase children eating burgers

I unwrap the sodden princess
He's still watching
        Skin and bone

My hands are blackened
               Paper and ink
His hands are outstretched
               Skin and bone

To those too crazy
To those too busy
Their hands are bloody
All those too greedy
For power and money
               Paper and ink.

*Sue Johns*
*Mitcham & Morden CLP*

## Justice

How good it will be
When you're out of a job Mr Major,
And the others around your feet!
When the coin turns to the other side,
And you're standing on the street.
Yet you will not be poor like some we know,
And they say revenge is sweet.

You cannot bring back the old who have died
From lack of care in the terrible Thatcher years,
And however much you may have tried
The babes who have ceased to endure
When no incubators could be found
And they watched them drown in tears.
When children sat in damp dark rooms
And looked through the roof to the sky.
And the old froze to death when the heat was cut off
While you slept through every lie.

You will never be poor Mr Major
However much tax you will pay.
We will have to wait for the line-up of blue
On that terrible judgement day!

*Marian Flanders*
*Newport West CLP*

## Nye Bevan Remembered

It was after the war
The last World War
When lovers were parted
Mothers and sons
And many watched their men go
Full of bravery and fated

Never to return.
When tales of horror seeped through daily
Of things being done to men by men;
And not just men
but women too, and worse than that
To children who had done no harm
And much, much more but then
I could go on......

And soldiers who died bravely fighting
Must have sometimes thought
"What am I doing here?"
And, as in war, that evil above all
The worst of man is seen and yet,
Even in the darkest place
Perhaps, were those whose humanity rose
Above the horror of it all?
There were many who returned no doubt
Whose scars were visible
And many whose were not.
Out of it all, paid with the blood of millions
Who really would have rather lived in peace
A change began......

A new determination that all men count
And each deserved his due
The NHS was founded
The dreams of many came true.
And you it was dear Nye who
Fought for the right for everyone
That NEVER AGAIN would money buy
Priority on Health.
And it was the finest thing
That ever was fought for
Freedom from want in the greatest need
When sick and ill.
How proud she must have been
Who stood beside, encouraging you.

It has been said
That when things changed
It broke your heart to see
And so...
You died
Before your time
And she lived on
To see that fight
Until more recently.
And that dream lives on today
We will not forget
your gift to us...
The dream that became
       Reality.

*Carol Pidgeon*
*Horsham  CLP*

## Labour's Gospel

I have reached my Autumn years
But I still remember Spring
When I dreamed the Dream of Youth,
Of changing everything –
When the gap between the wealthy
And the poor would but be slight
And the future of our children
Would be for ever bright,
When the sick, the old, the vulnerable
Would get the greatest care,
And the plight of being homeless
Would be extremely rare,
Where every human being
Would stand for lasting peace,
Where the slaughter of the innocents
Throughout the world would cease,
And the rich fruits of our lovely world
Were within everybody's reach.

A dream? No, Labour's Gospel --
"Each for all and all for each!"

*Joan Leahy*
*Lewisham East CLP*

# Typiclus Toriclus

Blue rinsed Jolly Roger,
Tory through and through,
Self first, self last,
Tough luck on you and you.

Typical BUPA associate,
Never in the queue,
But gets a pimple on the bum,
Then he'll leap ahead of you.

Pretends to be a Christian,
Who follows Christ the Lord,
But he forgets what Jesus did
To the money-making horde.

His solution for the jobless,
To get them off the dole,
Would be to close down all the pits
Then burn the men as coal.

He's a nauseous, bellicose Tory,
A sabre rattling nit,
A flag waving fanatic,
And a war-mongering twit.

He'd scatter the Asian community,
Repatriate the foreign horde,
But if this couldn't be arranged,
He'd put them to the sword.

But let's hope we find some justice
In this unfair scheme of life,
So in the event of reincarnation
He returns as Carl Marx's wife.

Then let's further hope he's conscious
As he shares the nuptual bed
Each night as he's carousing
He's consummating with a red.

*Peter Clark*
*Blyth Valley CLP*

## Topical Adaptation Of Rudyard Kipling's
## "If"

If you can keep your house while all about you
    Are losing theirs and being re-possessed,
If you can keep your job and work well too,
    Without the fear of being dispossessed,
If you can pay your bills and have the cash to spare
    For weekend breaks, romantic trips away,
Or little gifts to show how much you care,
    Yet still keep warm each freezing winter's day.

If you can plan and make your plans come true
    Yet somehow know the costs won't be a strain,
If you can proudly own a brand new car or two
    Yet still go by an inter-City train,
If your pound coins still fetch sufficient francs
    To buy a meal and wine for two in France,
Yet write off commission charged at banks
    Without a wince, a moan or second glance.

If you can take a loan to do a course
    And still be sure you'll never be in debt
Since Dad has savings that will soon be yours,
    And he would never wish to see you fret,
If you can keep ill health and age at bay
    And not go blind or suffer something worse,
Or if you can't, but know that you can pay
    To make quite sure that you are treated first.

If you can live your life without a child
    And stay in love with one who earns the same,
If you can see such strife and not get riled
    But just proclaim: 'They've got themselves to
    blame'
If you can cheat before you're cheated on
    And take what's theirs, and think it all good fun,
Yours is this world — I'm sure that you'll get on.
    What is more — you'll vote Tory my son.

*Bruce Nairne*
*Harrow East CLP*

199

# Party-Poet Cross Reference

*Note: The compiler has checked this list as far as practicable but it may not be entirely accurate*

| Party | Poet/s |
|---|---|
| Altrincham & Sale West CLP | Hilton, Anthony |
| Alyn & Deeside CLP | Wallace, Nina |
| Banbury CLP | Bogenschutze |
| Bassetlaw CLP | West, Larry |
| Beckenham CLP | Gwyer, Paula |
| Birmingham Hodge Hill CLP | Nicholls, Anne |
| Blaby CLP | Kaylor, Kenneth |
| Blackley CLP | Banks, Dorothy |
| Blackpool N & Fleetwood CLP | (the late) Owen, Jim |
| Blackpool South CLP | Reeves, Nancy |
| Blaydon CLP | Mood, Kenneth |
| Blyth Valley CLP | Clark, Peter |
| Bolsover CLP | Cooper, Glynis; White, Neil |
| Bolton N E CLP | Hayes, Christopher |
| Brent East CLP | Doyle, Sabrina |
| Brentford & Isleworth CLP | Cross, Beryl |
| Bridgwater CLP | Naylor, Mary |
| Brighton Pavilion CLP | Rose, Iain |
| Bristol NW CLP | Hall, Dorothy |
| Burnley CLP | Pinder, Bob |
| Canterbury CLP | Wallis, Olive |
| Carlshalton & Wallington CLP | Knight, Patricia |
| Chatham & Aylesford CLP | Saunders, Cyril |
| Chesham & Amersham CLP | Bligh, Joan |
| Chichester CLP | Ellis, Wendy |
| Christchurch CLP | Spack, Ron |
| City of Durham CLP | Moir, Jean |
| City of York CLP | Mumby, Linda; Finney, Fred; Yoell, Rebecca |
| Clwyd South CLP | Barford, Beth; Hamilton-Morris, Alexia |
| Colne Valley CLP | Dearnley, Mary |
| Crewe & Nantwich CLP | Kendall, Philip; Greger, Sonia |
| Croydon South CLP | Cardy, Jean |
| Derby North CLP | Horobin, Jill |
| Doncaster Central CLP | Colpus, Gwendoline |
| Dover CLP | Curry, Stan; McCabe, Edward |
| Dudley South CLP | Parkes, Richard |
| Dulwich & W Norwood CLP | Dixon Ward, Sylvia |
| East Devon CLP | Edmands, Gerry; Bateman, John |
| East Ham CLP | George, Mark; Leach, Frann |
| Edinburgh Central CLP | Rogers, Nellie; Barker, James |
| Edmonton CLP | Looker, Bill |
| Greenwich & Woolwich CLP | Warren, Sidney |
| Harrow East CLP | Nairne, Bruce |
| Hendon CLP | Celner, Tony; Moss, Jack |
| Hitchin & Harpenden CLP | Ross, Gavin; Campbell, Susan |
| Huddersfield CLP | Manning, Lin |
| Horsham CLP | Gregory, John; Clapp, David; Pidgeon, Carol |
| Ilford North CLP | Harvey, Jackie |
| Ipswich CLP | Hill, David; Painter, Clifford |
| Islwyn CLP | Harris, Roy |
| Kensington & Chelsea CLP | Hobday, Charles; Waters, Gerald |
| Kilmarnock & Loudoun CLP | Mackie, Annie |
| Leeds East CLP | Pearson, Roy |
| Leeds North West CLP | Riley, Patricia |
| Leicester East CLP | Snowden, Stuart |
| Leicester South CLP | Pullin, Mike |
| Leicester West CLP | Synclére, Ian |
| Leominster CLP | Challis, Ilse; O'Toole, Martin |
| Lewes CLP | Thorpe, Malcolm |
| Lewisham East CLP | Leahy, Joan |

| Party | Poet/s |
|---|---|
| Lincoln CLP | Frohock, Neville |
| Mansfield CLP | Banks, Rosemary |
| Medway CLP | Cox, Sylvia |
| Mid Norfolk CLP | Mason, Norman; Jeffery, Neil |
| Mid-Bedfordshire CLP | Hall, Peter |
| Mitcham & Morden CLP | Johns, Sue |
| Newark CLP | Carver, Barbara |
| Newcastle upon Tyne Central CLP | MacPherson, Billy |
| Newport West CLP | Flanders, Marian |
| North Cornwall CLP | Taylor, Byron |
| North Tyneside CLP | Kane, Dave |
| North West Cambridgeshire CLP | Rowe, Anthony |
| North Wiltshire CLP | Morgan, Ken; Reid, Michelle |
| Nottingham North CLP | Marson, Lawrence |
| Portsmouth South CLP | Somerville, Roy |
| Reading West CLP | Dearing, John |
| Reigate CLP | Tree, Arthur |
| Rother Valley CLP | Newton, Margaret |
| Ruislip - Northwood CLP | Turner, Mike |
| Runnymede & Weybridge CLP | O'Connell, Debbie |
| Saffron Walden CLP | Roberts, Paddy |
| Scunthorpe CLP | Prescott, Martha |
| Sedgefield CLP | Chaytor, David; Leng, John D |
| Sevenoaks CLP | Oakley-Hill, Robin |
| Sherwood CLP | Cowrie, E; Francis, Keara |
| Shrewsbury & Atcham CLP | Sayles, Patrick; Westall, Bill |
| Skipton & Ripon CLP | Smith, Joan |
| Slough CLP | Greene, Richard |
| Solihull CLP | Cook, Norman |
| South East Cornwall CLP | Bates, Sylvia |
| Southampton Test CLP | Davis, Stella; Northover, Kim; Risbrook, John |
| Southend West CLP | Criosdeagh Rhuadh |
| St Albans CLP | Singh-Toor, Stephen |
| St.Ives CLP | Wornes, Ray |
| Stafford CLP | Taylor, Derek Alan; Leese, Sheila; Palmer, Peter |
| Stevenage CLP | Levy, Linda |
| Stockton South CLP | Walmsley, Steve |
| Stoke-On-Trent North CLP | Terry, Andy |
| Stratford-on-Avon CLP | Bongilli, Joan; Corser, Anne |
| Stroud CLP | Ford, Norman |
| Tatton CLP | Ellis, Ron |
| Taunton CLP | Brumby, Robin |
| Teignbridge CLP | Blackman, Ben |
| Telford CLP | Hickman, C J; Atherton, Susanne |
| Torfaen CLP | Miller, Graham |
| Tunbridge Wells BLP | St.John, Terrence |
| Tynemouth CLP | O'Rourke, John |
| Wallasey CLP | Irving, Therese |
| Wansbeck CLP | Heslop, Helen |
| Wantage CLP | Wilkinson, Arthur |
| Warwick & Leamington CLP | Kendall, Denys |
| Wellingborough CLP | Majerski, Mona |
| Westbury CLP | Browning, Rosemary |
| Weston-super-Mare CLP | Meakin, Pamela |
| Windsor CLP | Chanan, Gabriel; Stonebridge, Bill |
| Wirral South CLP | Wood, Andy |
| Wolverhampton North East CLP | Gilbey, Madge |
| Wythenshawe & Sale East CLP | Shaw, Beryle |
| Yeovil CLP | Macille Mhoire |

# Topic Index

# Titles Index

# Titles Index (continued)

# Poet Index

# RE-ORDERING

Subject to availability further copies of this book may be ordered from the publisher. All proceeds will continue to be passed to the Labour Party until stocks are exhausted.

Do not send cheques with your order. If stock is still available, you will be sent a pro-forma invoice.

Written orders should be sent with a stamped addressed envelope please to:

> Derek Taylor,
> 7 Old Acre Lane,
> Brocton,
> STAFFORD ST17 0TW.

Alternatively you may telephone  01785 662257

Single copies will be charged at £7.50 plus £1.25 towards delivery.

To allow for local fund-raising and to encourage their use as raffle prizes etc. the the following discounts apply for more than one copy:

> 2 copies £14 plus £2.50 delivery.
> 3 copies £19.25 plus £3.75 delivery.
> 4 copies £22.00 plus £5 delivery.
> 5 or more copies £5 each plus (any quantity) £5
> delivery.